ECUMENICAL STUDIES IN WORSHIP

No. 2

WORSHIP IN THE CHURCH OF SOUTH INDIA

by

T. S. GARRETT, M.A.

*Lecturer at Tamilnad Theological College and Member
of the C.S.I. Synod Liturgy Committee*

LUTTERWORTH PRESS

LONDON

ECUMENICAL STUDIES IN WORSHIP

General Editors:

J. G. DAVIES, M.A., D.D.
Senior Lecturer in Theology, The University of Birmingham

A. RAYMOND GEORGE, M.A., B.D.
Tutor, Wesley College, Headingley, Leeds

Advisory Board:

PROFESSOR OSCAR CULLMANN
Universities of Basel and the Sorbonne

PROFESSOR H. GRADY DAVIS
Chicago Lutheran Seminary, U.S.A.

DR. F. W. DILLISTONE
Dean of Liverpool Cathedral, England

PROFESSOR ROGER HAZELTON
Pomona College, Claremont, California, U.S.A.

PROFESSOR J. KUMARESAN
Gurukul Lutheran College, Madras, India

REV. R. STUART LOUDEN
Kirk of the Greyfriars, Edinburgh

DR. ROBERT NELSON
Dean, Theological Faculty, Vanderbilt University, U.S.A.

CANON D. R. VICARY
Headmaster, King's School, Rochester, England

CONTENTS

First published 1958

COPYRIGHT © 1958, T. S. GARRETT

Lutterworth Press,
4 Bouverie Street, London, E.C.4

ACKNOWLEDGMENTS

Thanks are due to the Rev. H. K. Moulton, a member of the C.S.I. Liturgy Committee since it was first formed in 1948, for valuable criticism; to the Oxford University Press in India for permission to make many quotations from the C.S.I. services; and above all to fellow members of the Liturgy Committee, past and present (to whom this book should be dedicated), for work joyfully done together.

T. S. G.

Tirumaraiyur
4th February 1958

Printed in Great Britain by
Latimer, Trend & Co Ltd., Plymouth

I

THE CHURCH OF SOUTH INDIA
AT WORSHIP

THE FIRST OBJECT likely to catch the eye of someone entering a church in South India before the celebration of the Lord's Supper will be (if the recommendation in the introduction to the Order has been carried out) an alms dish, in which the worshippers are invited to place their offerings as they come in, and in which these will be presented later at the time of the offertory. As often as not, this "alms dish" will be a *chembu* or plain brass pot, such as can be bought by anyone from the brassmonger in the bazaar, identical in pattern and quality with the one that a woman uses to pour water on her child when giving him a bath beside the village well or to serve *rasam* (curried soup) to her hungry family. In such a vessel is the money which betokens man's daily work offered to God to be set apart for the fulfilment of His purpose. Indeed, some of the offerings, which will have to be set down beside the *chembu*, because they will not go into it, may well be the actual products of human labour; the first fruits of the plantain trees in the garden, the first egg that a pullet has laid, the first measure of milk from a newly purchased cow. These too may be taken up in the offertory procession, if those who have offered them have not preferred to lay them at the sanctuary steps beforehand.

All this is an illustration of what has now become a commonplace in liturgical studies and construction, namely that a living liturgy must grow out of the life of the worshipping community. How far, apart from the illustration just given, a proper relationship exists between South Indian society and the worship of the Church of South India must be judged as this book goes on. Part of the material for such a judgment must be some account—an all too brief one no doubt—of the kind of congregations whose worship has to be guided by the united Church and the way in which they live from day to day. To fail thus to sketch in the background, before proceeding to theological and liturgical points in our forms of worship, would be to display them without their relation to the people whom they most concern and leave ourselves open to the criticism that *The Order for the Lord's Supper* and other forms of service, though pretending to have had their birth in South India, are really a miscellany of foreign liturgical writings, fabricated in the theologian's or liturgist's study rather than emerging from South India's worshipping congregations. There may be considerable truth in this criticism, and those who have been engaged in liturgical construction in the C.S.I. would be the first to acknowledge it. However, there are, I believe, factors to the contrary, and it is to discover these that we turn to the life of the Church as it is.

First of all, although the C.S.I. in all its component denominational heritages is older and more strongly established than is the Church in most other parts of India, and although in Travancore it has an infiltration of those whose Christian ancestry goes back further than that of many Christians in the West, it is still a predominantly young Church, and Christians are as yet only a small minority in the midst of a passively resisting, if not actively hostile, non-Christian environment.

In this situation, so like that of the Church in the early centuries, there are inevitably varying degrees in which Christians find themselves up against or dominated by a world that knows not the true God. At one end of the scale is the place where there are hardly any Christians at all. An old student of the theological college where I teach, not long ordained when I recently visited him, had only a handful of Christians even at the headquarters of his pastorate, and of these the majority were Christian students who were doing a year's course at a government women teachers' training school near by and were therefore only temporary residents. Labouring, as they were, under the pressure of the "common worship" which is imposed upon them in these "basic" training schools—an anthology of purple passages from the Hindu and Muslim scriptures with the Beatitudes and the Lord's Prayer chanted in much the same way—the worship to which they came in the pastor's house had a vital significance for their faith and witness. The house church too sounded the apostolic note. Was the liturgy of the C.S.I. sufficiently "missionary" for such a congregation, declaring the Gospel as it obeyed its command? Was it too magnificent in its classical form for this homely atmosphere, or could its very classicality help to bring home to these isolated believers that they were participating in the worship of the universal Church?

Another more promising congregation, also looked after by one of my old students, is that of about a dozen families of leather workers, all recent converts. The necessity of their trade in a rural community gives them a status in society which is in some respects higher than that of several other groups, but in the Hindu caste system they are regarded as the lowest of the low. Yet a visit to them left one in no doubt that something had happened which had transformed their situation, giving them new corporateness and purpose, so that they were active in witnessing to their neighbours, and not only to those of their own community. Their pastor is the first of their people to be ordained. Problems there were, no doubt, in their common life, particularly those arising from the psychology of a suppressed people, the old Adam that still hangs about the convert's neck. What could the eucharistic liturgy mean to them? Perhaps rather, what an opportunity for them to take it and make their own contribution to it, particularly in view of their traditional, if somewhat barbaric, skill with the drum and other rustic musical instruments! And to see them perform their most popular folk dance taken and "baptized" without a break from their Hindu heritage, with the epic poem, which accompanied it in sing-song recitative, transformed from an account of the activities of a goddess into a proclamation of the Gospel, was to be prompted to the unorthodox question, why should they not have this dance in their liturgy? Their longer established Christian neighbours might well be scandalized at the thought.

It is to these that we must now turn, for the characteristic congregation of South India is one which may have been established fifty or more years ago and of which the majority of members have grown up from childhood in the faith. Illiteracy is steadily being banished from among them by the great national enterprise in education, of which Christian missions were the pioneers. But it is still sufficiently prevalent to make some measure of liturgical crystallization the norm even in congregations of a non-liturgical heritage. Such parts of the services as the congregation are expected to join in saying must be repeated in the same form Sunday by Sunday until they become familiar and eventually known by heart.

The Liturgy Committee in the drafting of the Church's orders of worship has clearly had congregations of this type in the forefront of its view. To such Christians the C.S.I. *Order for the Lord's Supper* has not come as something entirely new and "out of the blue". If they were formerly Anglicans, they will have been long familiar with an exact translation into their own language of the *Book of Common Prayer*, and in the Methodist Church of South India the Order for Holy Communion in use was practically identical with the Anglican.

To both these groups the new *Order for the Lord's Supper* must appear as but a development of the old. In the congregations of the former "South India United Church", comprising Congregationalists and Presbyterians, the Order for the Lord's Supper most commonly in use was not dissimilar to the first Order in the Congregationalist, *A Book of Public Worship*.[1] Although the points of resemblance between this and the C.S.I. order may be fewer than is the case with the Anglican rite, the C.S.I. order has had an unexpectedly enthusiastic welcome in congregations of this heritage. Perhaps they have sensed that in using it they are claiming a richness in worship which was not always present in the traditions in which they were brought up. By so doing they are certainly not exchanging freedom for chains. Already the presence of a now happily diminishing number of illiterates in their congregations had necessitated forms of worship more liturgical than those current in congregations of similar heritage in the West; while the many alternatives given at different points in the new orders of worship and the place accorded in them to extempore prayer, if desired, preserve in them the freedom of the Spirit for which those Churches that in England are called the "Free Churches" stand.[2]

Perhaps, then, we may be permitted to give at this stage a preliminary answer to the question which has already been raised: How far have the liturgical developments in C.S.I. emerged from the life of the worshipping community?

The answer would seem to be that they have a definite relationship to the worship which was practised in the uniting Churches at the time of union, and, although there has been no bargaining about it, each order of worship has turned out to be a happy blend of contributions from the different heritages. At the same time these varying contributions have been transcended, and a mere miscellany of existing practices avoided, by our aim of reappropriating the great classical tradition of Christian worship, as found in the ancient liturgies, while subjecting it to the critical insights of the Reformation.

On the other hand, we cannot but admit that the liturgical forms in use in South India, whether pre-union or post-union, are for the most part imported from the West, and that even those elements in them which have had their birth in India show marked signs of Western

[1] 2nd edit., 1949, p. 135.
[2] This title has, of course, no meaning in a country where all denominations are, from one point of view, "disestablished" and, from another point of view, are each by the principle of comity "established" in the area allotted to it for expansion.

influence. This applies as much to the liturgy of St. James, which has been our main source for the recapturing of the classical heritage, as to Protestant forms of worship, in spite of its centuries of use on South Indian soil by the Christians of St. Thomas.[1] In our borrowings from this liturgical heritage we should not delude ourselves into thinking that we are making our liturgy more indigenous, though a detail such as the form of the Greeting of Peace, which the C.S.I. has taken from the Syrian Churches of Travancore, may be of Indian origin.

It would not, however, be fair to the Churches in India to say that, because their forms of worship are for the most part foreign in origin, they have therefore remained equally foreign in character after a period of use in India. Like many other Oriental countries, India has a faculty of assimilating foreign elements into her culture while still remaining essentially Indian; and no one from the West who has lived and worshipped with the Church in India for any length of time would say that such externals as church architecture in which Gothic predominates, or an Anglican order of service, make the worship offered any less the Indian Church's own. Somehow an Indian atmosphere always succeeds in asserting itself. Where worshippers are seated on the floor, as they mostly still are in South India, and where Carnatic music and musical instruments are preferred to Western, there can be no mistaking this.

It is probably in such accessory elements of worship that the Indian spirit will continue to be most clearly manifest. In all the major Indian languages there has been Christian poetic creativity in the tradition of the great *bhakti* poets of Hinduism. The movement of preference for these "Christian Lyrics", as they are called, is gaining ground, as against the translations of Western hymns which were at one time so popular. Indeed, India's Christian lyrical tradition may one day be discovered by the world as a classical contribution to literature. On the other hand, India's liturgical creativity has been distinctly jejune. Booklets such as *Ashram Japamalai* and *An Offering of Worship from India*[2] have a winsome air of sensitive devotion about them, but can hardly claim to be in a great liturgical tradition. These two South Indian examples have been mentioned because English translations of

---

[1] For an account of the worship of these Christians see L. W. Brown, *The Indian Christians of St. Thomas*, 1956, pp. 213–288.

[2] Published by Christu Kula Ashram, Tirupattur (1950), and Livingstone Press (1950), respectively. The latter is the joint effort of women trainees at Attungal Bible School, Travancore.

them are available; but it would be difficult to find other original productions as yet untranslated, which are of acknowledged liturgical merit. Perhaps the genius of Indian Christian devotion, apart from its sterling expression in the lyrics, is best revealed in extempore prayer.

The foreigner who knows an Indian language can never fail to be inspired by the naturalness and grace with which many of the simplest of his Indian brethren offer prayer in their own words; but an impression of this is not easy to convey in other languages. For liturgical construction the Indian Church may well continue to be indebted in some measure to colleagues from the West, as has been the case with the liturgical developments of C.S.I. But this Western contribution has been gratefully accepted and not regarded as merely foreign. Where, as is mostly the case, it is based on the language and thought-forms of the Bible, it clearly transcends national differences and is part of the truly catholic heritage which Churches of all lands must claim as their own. Indeed the Indian Christian, with his predominantly rural background, is able to enter more easily into this heritage than his urbanized Western brother, so that an Indian congregation may be more at home with, say, the Anglican Prayer Book translated into their own language than a modern English congregation is with the sixteenth or seventeenth century original. At least the style and vocabulary is nearer to that of their own time in the former case than in the latter.

To end this chapter we must return to our survey of the different types of congregation found in the Indian Church. So far we have not mentioned the village in which the whole, or almost the whole, population is Christian. Such large Christian communities are at present rare, though the author happens to have been called to work in an area where there are several within a radius of ten miles. They are clearly the fruit of a movement of whole peoples towards Christian faith; and if we live in expectancy of the ultimate winning of India for Christ, our evangelistic strategy must be planned in the hope of the continued occurrence of such people's movements.

There is a tendency among such congregations to "sit at ease in Zion".[1] One misses in them that spirit so evident in the early Church which one should expect to find wherever Christians of the younger

[1] One of them, not far from the place of writing, rejoices in the name Jerusalem patnam, conferred upon it by the early Lutheran missionaries who were at the beginning of the nineteenth century employed by the Anglican missionary societies.

Churches are still a minority group. Yet here are Christian social entities which we must inevitably look to as the prototypes of the Indian Christian civilization of our hopes, even though we may pray that future fulfilment will far transcend present realization. Their significance for our liturgical development is surely that the meaning of worship as the dedication of human society to God should find a richer expression in them than elsewhere. The liturgical productions of C.S.I. should be adaptable—perhaps more adaptable than they are— to the worship of the smallest and most backward group of the faithful, in their manward aspect declaring God's Word to His people and binding them together in a fellowship of witness, and in their Godward aspect giving expression to the Church's fundamental faith and self-offering in a form which the simplest can comprehend. These liturgical forms should, however, also look to the future and be capable of being instruments for the declaration that all life has as its end consecration to God and is intended to be a sacramental instrument of His kingly rule. The revival of the classical heritage in our worship, with particular stress on its corporate character, so that all have a part to play in "doing the liturgy", has this aim in mind. Those who have taken part in *The Order for the Lord's Supper*, giving to each other the Greeting of Peace, following the offertory procession with their prayers and self-offering and, after receiving the effective signs of their participation in the body and blood of Christ, confirming their self-offering in the post-communion prayer, may well have been vouchsafed a vision of the Indian Church of the future as in this sacramental act bringing the glory of the nation to the throne of Grace.

II

THE LITURGY COMMITTEE AT WORK

IN *The Constitution of the Church of South India* the principle is laid down: "No forms of worship which before the Union have been in use in any of the uniting churches shall be forbidden in the Church of South India, nor shall any wonted forms be changed or new forms introduced into the worship of any congregation without the agreement of the pastor and the congregation."[1]

On the other hand, subject to this principle: "It is competent to the Synod of the Church to issue forms of worship to be used on special occasions, and regulations with regard to the essential elements or constituent parts of other services."[2]

In the section of the Constitution succeeding the one last quoted[3] a detailed synopsis of elements desirable in a service of Holy Communion is given. This subsequently proved of great value in giving direction to the compilation of *The Order for the Lord's Supper.*

It was clear, then, from the start that the Church of South India would have to appoint a liturgy committee to give advice and prepare resolutions for the Synod on points likely to arise concerning these regulations. The committee appointed by the first Synod which met at Madura in 1948 was no doubt regarded as the successor to the committee appointed in 1943 by the Continuation Committee of the uniting Churches to prepare the service of Inauguration which was used on September 27, 1947, and the experimental Ordination services which are only now in process of revision.[4]

While it was necessary to prepare an ordinal before union which could be accepted by all sections of the united Church from the inauguration, the Church at first had no intention of compiling any other orders of service for regular use. It was envisaged that the prin-

---

[1] Ch. II (Governing Principles of the Church), 12.
[2] *Op. cit.* X, 1.
[3] *Op. cit.* X, 2.
[4] Bengt Sundkler, *The Church of South India: The Movement Towards Union,* 1954, pp. 339 f.

ciple, already cited, of unity within variety would be maintained. Indeed, that principle still holds good in spite of later developments.

It was not long, however, before a new need was felt. In the newly-formed dioceses at meetings of diocesan councils, as well as at the meetings of the Synod, and on other major occasions when the heirs of different traditions were brought together, it was fitting that they should confirm their newly-found unity at the Lord's Table. But what order of Holy Communion should they use? No existing order could give satisfaction to all who participated. And so under pressure of this consciousness of a unity which transcended differences and of the general demand to which it gave expression, the Executive Committee of the Synod asked the Liturgy Committee to prepare an Order for the Lord's Supper to be used in the first instance at the second Synod which was to meet in January 1950.[1] At the same time the drafting of an Order for Confirmation was commissioned. Thus the process of liturgical creativity was started which has been described as one of the main "growing points of the united Church".

Dr. Marcus Ward when he described the Liturgy Committee as "for the most part liturgically illiterate"[2] may have been indulging in epigrammatic exaggeration. As a member of the Committee at the time of writing he was doubtless passing a humble judgment on himself, and the rest of us should doubtless be equally humble in accepting the judgment. At least two who have taken a prominent part at various times in the Committee's deliberations had acquired, before they took up their task, some specialized knowledge of particular branches of liturgical study; but in Churches whose councils can bring a heavy artillery of liturgical scholarship to bear on the revision of their formularies the liturgists might well have raised their eyebrows, had they taken the trouble to spy out our lack of credentials and training. However, what we lacked in knowledge we made up for in enthusiasm, some of it inspired by the timely publication of Dix's *The Shape of the Liturgy*, an undoubted *praeparatio liturgica* for the Church of South India, albeit one which we hope we have taken with a grain of salt.

---

[1] L. W. Brown: "The Making of a Liturgy", *Scottish Journal of Theology*, IV, 1951. This journal has from time to time published reports of the Liturgy Committee's progress. See also J. R. Macphail: "Doing Over a Liturgy", VII, 1954, and T. S. Garrett: "Baptism in the Church of South India", VIII, 1955, I am indebted to these essays for several points in this and the following chapters.

[2] *The Pilgrim Church*, 1953, p. 130. As well as being the history of the first five years of C.S.I., this book gives in Chapter VII a valuable account of the early liturgical developments.

Not a few of us have acquired a considerable amount of liturgical knowledge *ex nihilo* in the course of undertaking the projects set us, and we have sometimes reflected whimsically that our not being liturgists of profound learning may possibly have saved us from having liturgical bees in our bonnets. At least we have come to regard liturgiology as the handmaid rather than the mistress of liturgi*ography*, which experience has taught us to be a distinct though related science.

Is all this rather unkind to the liturgical experts? We hope they will not take it so; for many of them have been very kind to us, putting their greater knowledge at our disposal and often entering with surprising ease into the spirit of the South Indian enterprise, even when they have not been entirely in sympathy with C.S.I.; not, that is, concerning themselves to advocate a particular liturgical standpoint, but understanding our aim of transcending the heritages. The study of liturgy, it seems, tends to produce a salutary cross-bench outlook, even among those of "catholic" upbringing, and liturgists of the Anglo-Catholic school have been amongst the most helpful, as they are in general the most informed. My colleagues in the Liturgy Committee will, I know, not mind my selecting them for special commendation, even though I be an ex-Anglican. We have got past that kind of partisanship. Doubtless liturgies have made us cross-bench too, though it was not always so. L. W. Brown (now Bishop of Uganda), in an article published in 1951,[1] mentions strong division of opinion between those of the Reformed tradition and those of the Anglican over the form of the offertory and the nature of the eucharistic sacrifice, as well as concerning what should be done with the consecrated elements after communion. Somehow those fences seem to have been reduced in height with the passage of time and our growth in mutual understanding.

The composition of sacramental Orders is as much a theological task as a liturgical one. There have always been several members of the Committee competent to judge the theological issues involved, though here too we have been readily afforded expert open advice from many parts of the world, and the theologians who have helped us have been wider in their range of ecclesiastical background than the liturgists.

A reader of our present list of members and their addresses, which is not very different in representation from previous lists, might well wonder why the staffs of theological colleges were more strongly represented than the parochial ministry. And if he agreed that we must

[1] See p. 13, n. 1.

draw in all those available with technical knowledge, he might still question the absence from the list of twenty-five (of whom twelve are "corresponding members" with a right to attend the meetings of the committee if they can find their own travelling expenses) of all but one layman and one woman. The difficulties encountered by those responsible for nominating suitable people for election by the Synod are considerable. Certainly the episcopal members of the Committee with their experience of conducting services in parishes of every type often represent their people better than the laity could themselves and save us from liturgical ventures which are technically admirable but pastorally inadvisable. In any case the limitations and omissions in our membership are in a measure counterbalanced by the fact that many of the most important criticisms and suggestions come from the diocesan liturgy committees, where presbyters in charge of pastorates and the laity are well represented. All the drafts of services are submitted to the dioceses before they are presented to the Synod Liturgy Committee. Recently a draft for Morning and Evening Prayer was prepared by a diocesan liturgy committee on the initiative of our one layman and presented by him to the Synod Committee, though it has not yet reached its final form.

This procedure is typical of the one we have generally adopted. A member of the Committee is asked to undertake the task of drafting. He produces a draft in consultation with local committees or with ad hoc groups, often composed of members either of the Synod or diocesan liturgy committees who find themselves taking a holiday at the same hill station. The preliminary drafts are often revised after criticism by a number of correspondents before they are presented to the Synod Committee by the person responsible for drafting.

This wider liturgical activity both keeps the Synod Committee in touch with the reactions of the Church as a whole to its work and also ensures a body of prayerful study and interest, without which a movement of liturgical renewal in the Church would be impossible.

The dioceses are also represented on a liturgy committee for each linguistic area. Hitherto its function has been mainly to provide agreed translations for the C.S.I. services as they have appeared in English. This is the only language common to all who have received higher education in India. The desirability of having universally accepted orders for Baptism, Holy Communion, Confirmation and Ordination has made it unavoidable that the originals of these orders should be in English, though the Committee has always endeavoured to keep the idiom of the South Indian languages in mind in its choice of words and phrases, and the principle has of late been emphasized that in translation priority should be given to the style and idiom of the language into which the translation is being made, rather than to a literal rendering of the original. The Indian translations are, of course, of much more importance, in that they are much more frequently used, than the English editions. They should therefore be accorded at least an equal status with them. Moreover, there has been a strong plea, which has received the provisional approval of the Synod Committee, that in the case of other forms of public worship and the occasional services, more work should be done in the different linguistic areas and greater freedom given to each area to devise its own forms. It is to be hoped that this will lead to fruitful development and stimulate the latent Indian liturgical genius.

III

AN ORDER FOR THE LORD'S SUPPER
OR
THE HOLY EUCHARIST

IF I MAY be permitted to begin this chapter with a note of personal reminiscence, my mind goes back to the first occasion on which I had the privilege of celebrating the Eucharist according to this rite. I was present at the Commission on Intercommunion appointed by the World Conference on Faith and Order which met in 1950 to prepare for the Lund Conference. Although I was only a substitute for the regular C.S.I. member, the officers of the Commission decided that the most satisfactory way to give opportunity to those members who wished to meet together at the Lord's Table was to ask the C.S.I. presbyter present to celebrate and to invite the others to partake. *The Order for the Lord's Supper* had not then been published, and I had only one copy of the somewhat inadequately printed draft which had been presented to the Synod in January of that year. We cyclostyled an outline of the Order and such of the people's parts as were not already familiar from other liturgies, and I was given half an hour at the end of a Saturday evening's session of the Commission before the celebration on Sunday morning to expound this rite, with which I myself was not as yet very familiar. An Anglican took the part of "deacon", and members representing various denominations read the lections and took part in the offertory procession. In spite of the handicap of unfamiliarity, an Anglican liturgist who was present remarked that this was perhaps the best liturgy in Christendom. I have no wish to substantiate this passing judgment against other claims. Comparisons are odious! But it doubtless represents the impression of not a few who have come to the C.S.I. Order for the first time, that a new star has arisen in the realm of liturgy.

It is not surprising that the Liturgy had been liked well enough when it was first used at the Synod and had been authorized "for optional and experimental use on special occasions", the cautious implication of this being that normally the congregations would continue to receive communion according to the orders to which they had been accustomed, former Anglicans and Methodists using almost identical editions of the Order contained in the *Book of Common Prayer*, and former members of the South India United Church (an earlier union of Presbyterians and Congregationalists) that contained in their *Directory of Worship*.

The original plan was to reconsider this experimental edition at the Synod of 1952; but things move slowly in India. The translations into the Indian languages had not long been published, so that the majority of congregations had not yet found occasion to use it. The experimental edition was therefore given another two years. In January 1954 a revised edition was "approved for general use wherever it is desired". Since then it has been steadily making its way. It is in regular use in all dioceses at ordinations, diocesan councils and other diocesan occasions. In many Churches of Methodist, Presbyterian, and Congregationalist origin it is now well established as the normal use, and though former Anglicans have shown a sturdier loyalty to their traditional formularies, there can be few congregations where occasional celebrations according to the new rite have not taken place. In one well-established congregation, consisting of an entire village of over three thousand souls, strong protest was at first registered against the proposal to introduce even occasionally the C.S.I. Order. When, however, a deputation from the Protestant Episcopal Church of America was received in 1956, a monthly use of the C.S.I. Order had already been accepted and the deputation was told in an address of welcome that it contained "the best consecration prayer in the world". The pattern of progress in the use of the other C.S.I. rites is not likely to be very different from this.

What then of the revision to which we have already referred as having been accepted by the Synod in 1954? The work of drafting the experimental edition had been done by the person responsible for compiling the draft in consultation with small groups and with a larger number of people by correspondence. It had been passed fairly rapidly in the full session of the Committee. Since its publication a number of comments had been received both from within India and from abroad on the basis of which a revised draft had been prepared. It was decided to devote the session of the Committee in September 1953 to a critical examination of this. J. R. Macphail, who had taken over the convenership from L. W. Brown after the latter had become Bishop of Uganda, writes:

"The recommendations that emerged, all of them unanimous, came

18

as a surprise to the members themselves. Most of us expected, I think, that we should produce a new Liturgy, and many of us had axes of our own to grind. We thought that something would happen when the Liturgy was scrutinized in committee. . . . But as we settled to our task, with a lot of homework behind us, we came to be more and more convinced that the pattern or structure of our Liturgy had weathered well; time and again, after we had exhaustively considered some big change, this way or that, we found that 'our end was our beginning', and we were well content to make a few verbal emendations."[1]

The most considerable changes made were: (1) the transfer of 1 Corinthians 11: 23-29, the Ten Commandments, Our Lord's Summary of the Law, and the Exhortation (adapted from the United Basel Mission Liturgy) from the place that they had occupied before the Confession, to a "preparatory service", intended to be used before a celebration of the Lord's Supper. Though it was not obligatory to read all these passages at this point in the eucharistic order, experience had shown that the service was often made unduly long and its movement arrested by their inclusion, though it is still permissible to read one or more of them before the Confession, if desired. (2) The Invitation to confession was rewritten to allow for a period of silent self-examination. (3) The latter part of the Confession, and (4) the Ordinary Preface were rewritten. Perhaps all these come under the category of verbal emendations, as no important doctrinal or liturgical issue was involved. The few other alterations in the text of the Order were of a very minor nature. We had, however, to devote some attention to the rubrics and it is hoped that the result has been to clarify them—always a difficult task until it has been discovered by experience what the minister and congregation actually do in their efforts to follow them.

At the same session of the Liturgy Committee the Order for the Lord's Supper was completed by the provision of *Bible Readings and Collects for Sundays and other Special Days with Proper Prefaces* (1954). We had temporarily used the lectionary of the *Indian Liturgy* (an Anglican production based largely on the Liturgy of St. James), but had decided that for various reasons we could not continue to follow this as it stood.

We must now turn to the text of the order.[2] As we have noted,

---

[1] *Scottish Journal of Theology*, VII, 1954, p. 377.

[2] Revised edit., 1954. *The Liturgy of the Church of South India*, by T. S. Garrett, 2nd edit., 1954, gives a fuller introduction to and commentary on the service than is possible here.

material is provided for use in a preparatory service, though wide liberty is given as to the form which this service should take. Opinions differ as to whether it is better to hold it the night before or when the congregation is gathered for the celebration with only a brief interval between the two.

In the opening procession of *The Order for the Lord's Supper*, which may take place during the singing of a hymn or psalm, the ministers come to the Lord's Table, one of them carrying the Bible from which the lessons are to be read. This is placed either on the Table or on a lectern. Those acquainted with the Byzantine liturgies will see in this an echo of the "Little Entrance", when the Gospel Book is carried in procession. Our more immediate exemplar has been the similar custom prevalent in the Church of Scotland. It marks the beginning of "the Ministry of the Word" which, as in the ancient liturgies, constitutes the first part of the service and is the necessary preparation for the administration of the sacrament.

There is a rubric that "the presbyter may stand behind the Table, facing the people". The structure of the eucharistic table in the ancient basilicas proves this position to have been the normal one in the early centuries of the Church's worship. Its revival has been much advocated by the Roman and Anglican Liturgical Movement. Here modern liturgical thinking and the practice of many of the Churches of the Reformation are at one. When the Presbyter thus faces the people, the notion of God's being "out there" beyond the east window is avoided and our Lord's words, "where two or three are gathered together in my name, there am I in the midst of them", are given added meaning.[1] It has not, however, been possible to make this position obligatory, owing to the structure of the eucharistic tables in some churches and local sentiment in favour of the eastward position.

The entrance is followed by the preparatory Collect for Purity, familiar to Anglicans and Methodists. The congregation have been standing and break forth into the singing or recitation of the "*Gloria in Excelsis*". This ancient hymn, which begins with the Angels' song at the birth of Christ and the Church's participation in that adoration, leads on to the plea for mercy and peace before "the Lamb of God, who taketh away the sin of the world". Our praise of God in His holiness and love thus naturally moves on to conviction of sin. This prepares the way for the confession which follows.

[1] See Basil Minchin, *The Celebration of the Eucharist facing the People*, 1954, for a fuller study and justification of this position.

Alternative to this is the *Trisagion*, *"the constant praise of the Jacobite Church"*:[1]

> Holy God,
> Holy and mighty,
> Holy and immortal,
> Have mercy on us.

It is right that we should be permitted to join in this act of adoration hallowed by ancient use in India. A still further alternative is the "Liturgy of the Lamb", i.e. three verses from the Book of Revelation read by the minister with the response "Unto the Lamb be glory", and a final congregational response in the words of the celestial hymn from the same source: "Salvation unto our God . . ."[2]; or another hymn may be sung.

Many may wonder whether the plethora of alternatives here and elsewhere in our services is likely to engender confusion. Experience has not shown this to be the case, the tendency being perhaps too often to choose the first of the alternatives. In this instance the *ethos* of the C.S.I. in bringing together many different heritages is indicated by the fact that the *Gloria in Excelsis*, though originally written in Greek, has mainly Western associations, the second is Eastern with an ancient Indian Christian tradition behind it, the third is one of those many biblical acts of worship characteristic of the reformed Churches. It may well be argued, and we have proceeded on this assumption, that the New Testament reveals a worship developing within liturgical framework and order, but with the freedom of the Spirit, and that the later more rigid crystallization of the liturgies was a bondage from which those Churches of the Reformation which repudiated it were right to free themselves, even if some went too far in rejecting liturgy as a whole. We hope we have struck a right balance between these two antithetical positions.

Confession and Declaration of Forgiveness come rightly at this point, and it will be seen that there has been an imaginative rehandling of traditional material. The main structure is taken from the Anglican rite, but there is a new presentation of it. The invitation to Confession, though it included some of the well-known phrases, has been re-written and divided into two parts, so as to include a period of silent self-examination. The form of Confession printed is taken with some

---

[1] L. W. Brown, *The Indian Christians of St. Thomas*, 1956, p. 218.
[2] Revelation 7: 10, 12.

revision from the alternative order for Holy Communion in the *Book of Common Order* of the Church of Scotland. It is admirable in its simplicity and directness and is generally used, though alternative forms of Confession are permitted. Next come the "comfortable words",[1] now introduced by "Hear the gracious Word of God to all who truly turn to him through Jesus Christ", printed in the Revised Version and without further introductory "Hear also . . .", the implication being that all belong to the biblical Word of God and we do not wish to bind ourselves to assertions of authorship which biblical scholarship may question.

The biblical declaration of forgiveness comes rightly before the presbyter, as God's representative to His people, pronounces the Church's form of declaration. Here, however, we have a theological and liturgical difference in our heritages which has not as yet been resolved, the Anglican heritage making use of a priestly absolution addressed to the congregation, the non-Anglican preferring a prayer to God for forgiveness in which the presbyter more clearly identifies himself with the people. As in other instances where we have agreed to differ within our united life, the C.S.I. has allowed both traditions to continue side by side; so that here the presbyter may say "us" and "our" for "you" and "your". If so, the prayer precedes the reading of the Gracious Word of God, which comes as the divine response to human penitence. The section concludes with the joyful response of the people "Amen. Thanks be to God."

The Ministry of the Word of God which follows is the culminating point of the first part of the service. To mark the fact that a new stage in the service has been reached, the mutual greeting of presbyter and people (no doubt of Jewish origin) is given:

> The Lord be with you;
> And with thy spirit.

This symbolizes the fact that celebrant and worshippers are united in Christ as they join in the liturgical act. The other great point at which this greeting is appropriately used is immediately before the *Sursum Corda*.

The Collect and Lections for the day come next. In the present stage of liturgical development in which we find ourselves, these have had

---

[1] The word "comfortable" has, of course, lost its old meaning in modern English.

to be published separately in two booklets.[1] But it will be convenient to give some account of them at this stage. We have followed Roman and Anglican tradition in adopting a calendar of the Church's year with variable collects and lectionary, but were not content to adopt the calendar or lectionary of any communion as it stood and without examination. Our first task was to provide collects and lections for use at celebrations of the Eucharist on Sundays and other major holidays (Christmas, Epiphany, Ash Wednesday, Holy Week, Ascension), which we were agreed should be generally observed. The Committee decided to simplify the calendar by dividing the year into three seasons—Christmas, Easter and Pentecost—and designating the other Sundays as before or after these great festivals, though the names Advent, Epiphany and Lent also appear in the Calendar.

The experimental edition of this was prepared by the Committee in 1953 and passed by the Synod in 1954. At the same time *Daily Bible Readings* was published, this being a lectionary of passages mostly shorter than existing ones, for use either at public services of Morning and Evening Prayer or for private reading. But the task was not complete, and at the Synod of 1956 the *Additional Bible Readings and Collects* were adopted. Thus C.S.I. accepted the principle of commemoration of the Saints on special days.

The traditional days for the remembrance of the more important apostles, together with the martyr Stephen and the evangelists, are included, though John is remembered on May 6 rather than December 27. January 1 is called "The Day of the Covenant". The Presentation of Christ in the Temple and the Annunciation are observed, as also the days of John the Baptist, Mary Magdalene, the Transfiguration and All Saints. A local festival, September 27, the date of the inauguration of the Church of South India, has been put on the same level with these. There are also collects and lections for national occasions, meetings of the Synod, diocesan councils etc., and the harvest thanksgiving, an occasion which has characteristically become a major festival in the rural Churches of India.

The question of other commemorations has been considered, but we have not yet been able to agree on a calendar of lesser special days to include the great figures and events both of ancient and modern Christendom and in particular the pioneers, builders and martyrs of

---

[1] *Bible Readings and Collects for Sundays and other Special Days, with Proper Prefaces* (1954), and *Additional Bible Readings and Collects for Sundays and other Special Days* (1956).

the Indian Church. At present we have published in this second booklet some "common forms", i.e. collects and lections which may be used at the discretion of the local church for the remembrance of names not included in the shorter list which corresponds to the ancient "red-letter days". Ten different collects and sets of lections are given under the headings: Apostles, Martyrs, Faithful Women, Evangelists, Pastors, Teachers of the Young, Teachers of the Church, Healers of the Sick, Prophets and Reformers, Servants of the Church. It should not be difficult to fit any "saint" into one of these categories, and it is perhaps as well to allow considerable elasticity of observance at present, so that the local churches may decide for themselves whom they wish to commemorate as powerful witnesses for Christ in former generations.

Additional Bible Readings and Collects also completes the Sunday lectionary by providing readings for Evening Prayer which had not been ready for publication in 1954. An annual lectionary is published which brings together the readings from all three booklets.

To return to the reading of the Bible in *The Order for the Lord's Supper.* The reading of the Old Testament follows the Collect and is followed by the people's response, "Thanks be to Thee, O God". A psalm or hymn may make the transition from the Old Testament to the New. Then follow the Epistle and Gospel with the responses "Thanks be to Thee, O God" and "Praise be to Thee, O Christ", respectively. The people may stand for the reading of Scripture, or at least for the reading of the Gospel.

As an example of the way in which traditional material has been combined with new in the selection of collects and lections we may take those chosen for the Twenty-first Sunday after Pentecost. As for other Sundays, a common theme is given as a title. In this case it is "The wretchedness and greatness of the Church". The Collect is an Anglican one, though transferred from another Sunday: "Lord, we beseech thee to keep thy household the Church in continual godliness. . . ." The lections are Amos 3: 1, 2; 1 Corinthians 3: 10–17; Mark 8: 27–35.

The sermon is obligatory and immediately follows the reading of Scripture; for it is the duty of the minister to bring the Word of God spoken of old into living relation with the present. This is the sequence of the most ancient liturgies and can be traced back as far as Justin Martyr in the second century. At that time, of course, the Creed was not recited in the eucharistic liturgy; so we have no precedent to guide us in our placing of it after the Sermon rather than before it, as in the Anglican rite. But the order we have adopted seems the more natural one. The Creed thereby becomes the declaration of the Word by the Church in response to the hearing of it in Scripture and preaching. While the Nicene Creed is the one printed and normally recited, there are still many congregations with a large number of illiterates who would have difficulty in learning it and still greater difficulty in understanding it. The Apostles' Creed is therefore allowed as an alternative.

The announcements which follow should not be regarded as just an inevitable interruption to the service, but as relating the common life of the Church to its worship. They will doubtless contain topics for which special prayer is asked and therefore come fittingly before the intercessions.

The question as to when the collection of alms should take place presented a minor problem to the Committee. We have already noted[1] the practice which is becoming increasingly common of placing a receptacle at the door of the church in which the worshippers place their offerings as they enter. This manner of collection, as well as approximating to primitive use, can be a more prayerful and self-dedicatory action than the handing around of a bag with or without the accompaniment of a hymn. But many congregations still prefer the latter for various practical reasons and we could hardly forbid them their preference.

Failing the use of the alms dish at the door, the most appropriate time for collection, when all present are communicants, is immediately before the offertory procession. But non-communicants may leave before this. It is therefore permissible to take the collection before the intercessions, and it is presented together with the offering of bread and wine at a later stage in the service.

Having begun by offering God our praise and adoration, having realized our sinfulness and made our confession to Him and having heard His word of reconciliation and redemption, it is right that we should go on to offer our intercession for the Church and the world.

This is perhaps a suitable point at which to note the part of the "deacon" in the service. The title has been put in inverted commas, because, as often as not, he is not in deacon's orders, but may be either another presbyter who is assisting the celebrant, or a layman. C.S.I. has been inquiring into the functions of a deacon in the Church, and if we should move away from the rather unsatisfactory tradition in

[1] P. 5.

which the diaconate is but a stepping-stone to the presbyterate and adopt instead a permanent diaconate with functions differing in some respects from those at present expected of deacons, it may well be that every Church will have one or more actual deacons to take their part in the liturgy.

The "deacon" has already come to the Lord's Table with the celebrant, probably carrying the Bible from which the lections are read. We have not laid down any precise regulations as to where he should stand. The working out of this can be left to the local churches and it is probable that a different use in this and other minor details will develop in a congregation of Anglo-Catholic origin from that which will be found amongst the heirs of the Congregationalist tradition. We are not interested in uniformity, but in unity.

The deacon has also led the people in the general confession and other parts assigned to the people. He may have read one or more of the lections, though other members of the congregation, men or women, may do this. At a later point in the service he will receive the bread, wine and alms and present them to the celebrant at the Table. His part is similar to that of the deacon in the Eastern Liturgies. He is both the assistant of the celebrant and the representative of the people and, besides having particular actions assigned to himself, helps to link the worship of all into a single liturgical unity.

It is the deacon now who leads the intercessions, unless the presbyter chooses to offer intercessions in his own words. This is the point at which extempore prayer finds a rightful place, if desired, in accordance with our assertion of the freedom of the Spirit. But more often than not the deacon, preferably kneeling in the midst of the people, reads one of the two printed Litanies of Intercession and the people respond.

The first Litany was taken with minor adaptations from a form of the Anglican rite authorized for use in the Diocese of Colombo. The suffrage, "That it may please thee that through thy heavenly benediction we may be saved from dearth and famine and may with thankful hearts enjoy the fruits of the earth in their season", is a reminder that failure of the crops is a danger which often threatens our rural congregations.

The second alternative is a selection of suffrages from the litany in the *Holy Qurbana*, or Syrian Liturgy of St. James, as used by the Indian Christians of St. Thomas. The actual form printed is closely similar to that found in the Prayer Book of the Episcopal Church of Scotland

and now in the *Proposed Prayer Book* of the Church of India, Pakistan, Burma and Ceylon. It was first used in the C.S.I. at the Inauguration Service on September 27, 1947. Since then a few changes have been made to bring its petitions more closely into relation with the common life of the Church. The intercessions conclude with one of two collects (taken from the *Book of Common Prayer*) read by the celebrant. The former stresses God's foreknowledge of our needs and the latter sums up our petitions "for all estates of men" in the Church.

The Pauline Benediction of 2 Corinthians 13: 14 marks the end of this first part of the service. It is right that those not yet of communicant status, if they leave now, should receive a blessing before they go and that the Liturgy of the Word should be thus concluded.

IV

THE LORD'S SUPPER (continued)

WE NOW COME to the great action of the Sacrament, corresponding to the Liturgy of the Faithful in the ancient liturgies.

First of all there is the offertory, which is far more than the taking or presenting of the collection. It includes the offering of the bread and wine which are to be set apart in accordance with our Lord's command. Both the money and gifts in kind of the collection and the bread and wine are the products of man's daily labour and therefore symbolic of his whole life. All stand to show that they thus associate themselves with the gifts which are being offered.

The action begins with the offertory sentences:

Presbyter: Behold, how good and joyful a thing it is, brethren, to dwell together in unity.

We who are many are one bread, one body, for we all partake of the one bread.

People: I will offer in his dwelling an oblation with great gladness, I will sing and speak praises unto the Lord.

It is only in union with Christ in His self-offering and within the fellowship of the Church which is His Body that we can make an offering acceptable to God.

It is right that at this point we should make known our brotherly love by significant action. Here, therefore, the ancient greeting known as "The Peace" may be given. In the early Church it was a kiss (see I Thessalonians 5: 26 and elsewhere in the New Testament, as well as the early liturgies). This is in accordance with Jesus' teaching in Matthew 5: 23, 24. We can only worship God rightly if we are reconciled to our brethren. In the worship today, even of the ancient Churches, the Peace has survived only as a verbal greeting of the celebrant to the people and in some cases a salutation amongst the clergy. But the Indian Christians of St. Thomas have through the ages preserved the tradition of passing the greeting from the ministers to the people and the people from one to another throughout the congregation. They have modified the form to make it a rather more intimate variety of the ordinary South Indian social greeting, and C.S.I. has followed their example. As the introduction to *The Order for the Lord's Supper* prescribes: "The giver places his right palm against the right palm of the receiver, and each closes his left hand over the other's right hand."[1] It is suggested that each person, as he gives the Peace to his neighbour, may say in a low voice, "The peace of God" or "The peace of God be with you".

A hymn is now sung and the offertory procession takes place. It is recommended that lay people should bring in the gifts. The deacon and other assistants, if any, receive the gifts and pass them on to the celebrant. While all remain standing, and the bearers of the offertory remain before the table, the celebrant reads the Offertory Prayer, echoing the Prayer of the Veil in the Liturgy of St. James, recalling "the new and living way to God's throne of grace" which Christ's death has opened for us (Hebrews 10: 19–25), and acknowledging that what we give to God already belongs to Him.

The offertory procession disperses and ministers and people fall to their knees to say together a very moving little prayer, as a preparation for that which is to come.

> Be present, be present, O Jesus, thou good High Priest, as thou wast in the midst of the disciples, and make thyself known to us in the breaking of the bread, who livest and reignest with the Father and the Holy Spirit, one God, world without end. Amen.

The prayer is inspired by a passage in the Mozarabic Liturgy, a "Gallican" form of the Western rite which had its origin in Spain, but it is an echo of a much earlier prayer, so primitive that Paul quotes it in Aramaic and does not translate it into Greek—*Maranatha*, "Lord, Come!" Was this in effect the first eucharistic consecration prayer uttered by the whole *ecclesia*? And does Paul's quotation of it,[2] after mention of the Kiss of Peace and what may be a fencing of the Table, indicate that it came at much the same point in the primitive eucharistic rite?[3] With us it declares that the laity are one with their minister as he proceeds, in accordance with our Lord's example and command, to take and bless and break and give.

And so in versicles and responses which are the common heritage of Christendom we lift our hearts to God on high and raise the paean of thanksgiving which is what the *anaphora*, or prayer of setting apart, is

---

[1] *Order for the Lord's Supper*, p. vii.   [2] 1 Corinthians 16: 22.
[3] See O. Cullmann, *Early Christian Worship*, 1953, pp. 12–20.

intended to be. In fact, the title approved by C.S.I. is "The Great Thanksgiving", rather than any of the traditional names.

It was no doubt right that we should choose to be conservative in this central part of the Liturgy and follow a classical pattern as well as using mainly traditional language. The Preface begins as in the Roman and Anglican rites. Its second clause, as printed in the text and read when no Proper Preface is appointed, begins "Through Jesus Christ, Our Lord . . ." as in the Western Prefaces; for all our thanksgiving is through Him. But it speaks of Christ as God's agent in creation and redemption in words which are in part borrowed from the anaphoras of the Liturgies of St. Mark and St. James. Once again this younger Eastern Church has a very proper link with the ancient Eastern Churches of Egypt and Syria. Of the eleven Proper Prefaces provided,[1] eight are from the *Book of Common Order* of the Church of Scotland, as being simpler and more easily understood by those unfamiliar with them than those known to Anglicans. The Prefaces for Easter, Pentecost and Saints' Days have been taken from the Prayer Book as proposed in 1928.

The *Sanctus* is sung or said by all throughout. This expansion of the song of the Seraphim in Isaiah's vision may well go back to the first century as a customary part of the eucharistic liturgy. The wording as we have it here has been taken unaltered from the *Book of Common Prayer*.

Again following an ancient tradition we echo the greeting of the crowds to Jesus as He rode into Jerusalem, but in the form found in the *Holy Qurbana*:

> Blessed be he that hath come and is to come in the name of the Lord. Hosanna in the Highest.

Our Lord's coming has more than one focus in time and we need to relate His coming in the Eucharist both to His coming of old and to His coming again.

As he begins the great prayer of thanksgiving, the celebrant takes up the praises which the people have just sung in the words "Truly holy, truly blessed art thou, O heavenly Father . . ." and continues in the words with which the parallel prayer in the Anglican rite begins, with the addition, however, of "to take our nature upon Him". This makes the passage a remembrance of the incarnation as well as of the atonement. The recalling of Christ's offering of Himself leads on directly to

[1] Printed in *Bible Readings and Collects*, pp. 21 f.

a remembrance of His command at the Last Supper and the reading of the narrative of the institution, during which the celebrant takes the paten and the cup into his hand. Thus the Church's faith in the atoning work of Christ is linked with His interpretation of His coming death as a sacrifice and His effective sign that His disciples should participate in it. The Eucharist has its setting in the sacrifice of Calvary, and its sacrificial significance depends upon the one oblation once offered.

The people again identify themselves with the actions and words of the celebrant by responding in words found in the *Holy Qurbana* at this same point:

> Amen. Thy death, O Lord, we commemorate, thy resurrection we confess, and thy second coming we await. Glory be to thee, O Christ.[1]

In the Eucharist, redemption through Christ as an event revealed in history and the hope of the Parousia are linked together and made dynamically real to the believing Church in the presence of the risen and living Lord to whom we ascribe all glory.

Next, and in its traditional place, comes an *anamnesis* or remembrance of Christ's passion, resurrection and ascension, linked with the expression of our obedience to His command to do this in remembrance of Him and a reiteration of our thanksgiving for redemption. This is followed by another response by the people of praise and thanksgiving taken from the *Holy Qurbana*. Again and again in this central prayer the meaning of *eucharistia*—thanksgiving—is made plain.[2]

[1] The last sentence in the Syrian form, which was adopted in the experimental edition, is "Have mercy upon us".

[2] Comment on *The Order for the Lord's Supper* in some Anglo-Catholic and Roman Catholic circles has been favourable, notably an article in the Spring number of *Istina*, 1955, by Fr. Louis Bouyer. But, partly in answer to this, a searching criticism of the C.S.I. in general and of *The Order for the Lord's Supper* in particular appeared in the *Eastern Churches Quarterly*, Spring 1956, by an Anglican priest, the Rev. W. Grisbrooke. As his strongest censure was directed against the C.S.I. *Anamnesis*, it is worth noting here:

(1) That Mr. Grisbrooke is mistaken in his assumption that the only sources to which the C.S.I. Liturgy Committee was indebted in the drafting of the service are those cited in the "acknowledgements". These were only made where necessary in view of copyright; the compilers studied a number of liturgies ancient and modern before the final draft was made.

(2) He fails to note that wherever the C.S.I. rite differs from its alleged sources —e.g. in the Offertory Prayer, the *Anamnesis* and *Epiclesis*—the change is towards a use of scriptural words and phrases. If these, as he maintains, are "considerably less susceptible of a Catholic meaning" than the forms found in various Anglican

31

The *Epiclesis* or invocation of the Holy Spirit is found in most ancient liturgies, though it is absent from the Latin Mass. The form in which we have accepted it does not imply a "moment of consecration" alternative to or complementary to the recital of the Words of Institution. As we have seen, consecration is best regarded as the setting apart with thanksgiving which takes place in the whole movement of the liturgy rather than in the repetition of any particular formula. The *Epiclesis*, then, declares our ascription of the divine action in the Eucharist to all three persons of the Trinity. Without such mention of the Holy Spirit our eucharistic prayer would be incomplete. As the New Testament teaches us, the Spirit guides us into all truth by taking the things of Christ and declaring them to the Church.[1] The Church's intention in celebrating the sacrament and the believer's faith in receiving it are therefore the work of the Spirit. Moreover it is by the Spirit that we grow together in the unity of the Church and look forward in hope to the completion of that unity and growth. The expression of that hope in the words of Ephesians 4: 13, 15 brings to a

liturgies and the order for Holy Communion in the *Book of Common Order*, the fault can hardly be laid at the door of C.S.I.! It is in the eucharistic teaching of the Bible that "catholic" and "protestant" can unite at the Lord's Table.

(3) The alternative theories of consecration, to one or other of which Mr. Grisbrooke would require us to adhere, are recognized by all scholars to be late. This particularly applies to the consecration of more bread and wine by recital either of the Words of Institution or the *Epiclesis* or of the whole consecration prayer. A much earlier practice which still prevails in the Eastern Churches is consecration of more wine, at least, by contact with the remainder of what has already been consecrated. It would be possible to interpret the C.S.I. provision for further setting apart according to this view; though C.S.I. has no intention of making such an interpretation binding. The words that may be said when setting apart more bread and wine are certainly not a formula of consecration. They declare the Church's intention in performing the action, and link the fresh bread and wine with the act of consecration which *has already taken place*, not by the recital of any particular formulae but by the whole movement of the liturgy from offertory to communion. And what is "consecration" but a setting apart with thanksgiving for sacramental use, so that Christ may be present and act in and through His sacrament? Our preference for the words "setting apart" rather than "consecration" is to emphasize the truth that, while man sets apart his gifts, it is God who acts and uses them.

(4) The chief weakness of the line of criticism we have examined is that it ignores the fact that the C.S.I. liturgy is more in accordance with the "catholic" liturgical tradition than any of the liturgies which C.S.I. has inherited from the uniting denominations. The interest of Fr. Bouyer's article lies in his appreciation of this fact.

[1] John 16: 14.

sublime close the eucharistic prayer of a Church which is pledged to work for ever larger and deeper union in a divided Christendom.

This prayer that the Holy Spirit may complete the unity of the Church is also a fitting prelude to our saying together "Our Father . . ." as fellow members of the household of God. We say it "boldly", as those who have received the Spirit of adoption through Christ.

And yet, together with the joy and freedom of our fellowship at God's board must go an acknowledgment that we are still sinners, "not worthy so much as to gather up the crumbs under God's table". And so, after silence to ponder on this and to prepare ourselves to receive the sacrament, we say together the Prayer of Humble Access, restored to the position for which it was originally intended by Cranmer, immediately before communion. One slight revision of the prayer has been made which has been deplored by some who love the cadences of the original, but which does not affect the translations into the Indian languages. The passage in question now reads:

> Grant us therefore, gracious Lord, so to eat the Flesh of thy dear Son Jesus Christ, and to drink His Blood, that our sinful bodies and souls may be made clean by His most precious Body and Blood.

The prayer as we know it in the Anglican Prayer Book is open to the misinterpretation that Christ's Body cleanses our bodies and His Blood our souls.

The Fraction, or breaking of the bread, has been restored to its original place immediately before communion. Its primary purpose is undoubtedly the practical one of distribution, but the Church has always seen in it a deeper symbolical meaning as signifying Christ's death and the fact that "we who are many are one bread, one body, for we all partake of the one bread".

The celebrant, as he breaks the bread, may say St. Paul's words of 1 Corinthians 10: 16, or else the phrase spoken in some ancient liturgies at the distribution, "the things of God for the people of God", or he may break the bread in silence.

There is a rubric in the Introduction (p. vii) that "Communion may be administered in the place and manner customary in the congregation". It is permissible, therefore, to use either the single cup of ancient tradition or the individual cups which have become the custom in many Free Churches. But the rubric goes on: "It is however recommended that communion may be given by 'tables', i.e. the people come forward to receive in front of the holy Table and each row remains kneeling till the presbyter dismisses them with a blessing such as 'The grace of the Lord Jesus Christ be with you all'." This is a contribution to the service from the Methodist heritage which has already become the normal C.S.I. use. Administration from the cup with a spoon, as in the Syrian Churches, has been introduced in some congregations, but on the whole has not been popular.

The words of administration printed in the text are:

> The body of our Lord Jesus Christ,
> The bread of life.
> The blood of our Lord Jesus Christ,
> The true vine.

Other forms of words are permitted (Introduction, p. viii). Indeed, the principle of unity in variety rather than uniformity is revealed most clearly in this part of the service. The *Agnus Dei* or some other hymn may be said or sung during the administration.

If the bread or wine set apart is insufficient, the formula for setting apart more is either, "obeying the command of Our Lord Jesus, we take this bread (wine) to be set apart for this holy use, in the name of the Father and of the Son and of the Holy Spirit. Amen", or the repetition of the words of institution. While the latter formula accords with Roman and Anglican use, the former is an adaptation of some words from the prayer of setting apart in the *Book of Common Order*. As we have already noted (p. 31 n.), it implies that consecration (or, as we prefer to call it, setting apart) has already taken place in the whole eucharistic action and that a fresh setting apart is performed by the taking up of more bread and wine into that action. Some form of words is needed to make clear the intention of the Church, as acting in obedience to Christ's command and in the name of the Triune God whose gift we receive, and the sole purpose of this formula is to provide such a clear statement of the meaning of the action.

When all have partaken, the celebrant calls the people to a final act of thanksgiving and self-oblation, saying: "Having now by faith received the sacrament of the Body and Blood of Christ, let us give thanks." Of the two alternative post-communion prayers, the first is a new composition based on scriptural passages, the second a conflation of the two alternative prayers in the *Book of Common Prayer*. In both cases there is thanksgiving for what we have received in the Eucharist and self-offering in the words of Romans 12: 1, 2. Cranmer's insight, to which he gave expression in the 1552 Prayer Book, that the eucharistic sacrifice is completed in our self-offering, after we have partaken of the effective signs of the self-offering of Christ, has thus been accepted and preserved.

The people may join in the post-communion prayer either vocally or silently. In either case they conclude with an ascription of blessing and glory to God in the words of Revelation 7: 12 and the celebrant gives the final benediction in the form taken from the Latin and Anglican rites. After this a hymn of praise or a part of Psalm 103, or the *Nunc Dimittis*, may be sung, during which the minister and his assistants return to the vestry carrying with them the Bible, the gifts of the people and the vessels used for communion. The final direction in the rubrics is that "any bread or wine set apart in the Service which remains over shall be carried out to the vestry, and may there be reverently consumed". Though there was variety of practice in this matter at the time of union, there is evidence that this way of completing the eucharistic action is now being widely accepted. It is regularly observed in the theological colleges of the C.S.I., and there can be little doubt that the generation of presbyters ordained within the united Church will come to regard it as the norm.

V

CHRISTIAN INITIATION—BAPTISM

WHILE THE FIRST edition of *The Order for the Lord's Supper* was still being drafted, a second task assigned to the Liturgy Committee was the drafting of *The Order of Service for the Reception of Baptized Persons into the Full Membership of the Church, commonly called Confirmation.* There was a pastoral reason for giving priority to the publication of this. While the variety of practice in the history of the Church and the different understandings of the meaning of Confirmation which have prevailed made it undesirable to impose uniformity at this final stage of initiation in the C.S.I., it is a fact of the first ten years of the united Church's history that episcopal Confirmation has spread to such an extent that it is regarded as the norm, not only in congregations of the Anglican heritage who adhere to it as strictly as in the past, but even in the majority of those congregations to whom episcopacy is something new. While it is not denied that the presbyter in charge of a congregation has the authority to admit members of his flock to communicant status, the appropriateness of the laying on of hands by the Bishop who represents the universal Church to the local church soon received wide recognition. There was therefore an urgent need for an order for Confirmation which would include other heritages than the Anglican. Baptism could wait; as the existing orders for the sacrament all contained the essential formula of Baptism with water in the name of the Trinity they could therefore continue in use as before. Thus the Order for Confirmation was published in 1950 and the Order for Baptism over four years later.

But we must consider them in their proper temporal sequence. Indeed, there was a certain awkwardness in their being drafted in the contrary order. It meant that the relation between the two rites was not fully considered. This has in a measure been remedied in *An Order for Holy Baptism* by a statement in the introduction that Baptism, Confirmation and first Communion are parts of one process of entry into the Church, and by a provision for the combination of these in one continuous rite, if desired, in the case of adolescent and adult candidates. But a more careful definition must await the forthcoming revision of the experimental editions of the two rites at present in use. For this reason the revision of the order for Confirmation has been delayed until it can be undertaken together with that of the order for Baptism.

The tremendous importance of the catechumenate in the early Church is well known and its revival in the younger Churches is an indication that they find themselves in much the same position as the early Church—a minority in the midst of a non-Christian world. Yet the decadence of what has been called "indiscriminate Baptism" can easily creep in amongst Christians of the second and later generations. The introduction to our order therefore devotes some space not only to rules for the instruction and approval of candidates able to answer for themselves, but also to asserting that parents or guardians should give due notice of their desire to bring their children to Baptism and should receive adequate instruction as to their responsibilities, particularly in the case of a first child.

The choice of godparents at Infant Baptism and of witnesses at Adult Baptism is welcomed as an ancient custom already observed in many congregations of the Church of South India; but emphasis is laid on the responsibility of the parents of the children to be baptized, and it is directed that they should make the responses in the service and that the godparents, if any, should make them with them.

There is a newly composed order of thanksgiving for childbirth to be said with both parents kneeling before the minister. First Psalm 103 or 116 is said or sung, and then the minister offers a prayer which is doubtless psychologically more satisfactory than the Anglican one in that it avoids the phrase "great pain and peril of childbirth". In any case the progress of maternity clinics and obstetric surgery in India, as elsewhere, demands a revision here.

The introduction also contains regulations for baptizing the sick and the administration of conditional Baptism. The first rubric of the service is: "The minister shall ascertain beforehand that the candidates have not already been baptized"—a necessary advice in view of the practice of some Adventist and Pentecostalist sects.

In Baptism, as in the Eucharist, there is a ministry of the word which precedes the ministry of the sacrament. This normally begins in our order with a hymn after which, as in the Church of Scotland rite to which this order is perhaps more indebted than to any other, the minister says: "Our help is in the name of Lord", and the people respond: "Who hath made heaven and earth." It is God who acts in every sacrament and the Church's action is only in supplication to Him and in obedience to His command.

The ministry of the word must include the message of the Old Testament as foreshowing the New, as well as of the New itself. No single lection from the Old Testament would be entirely satisfactory, and in any case, we can hardly avoid following the example of the apostles Peter and Paul in treating the Old Testament typologically in reference to Baptism. We have therefore at this point taken as our pattern the Lutheran and Anglican rites in giving expression to the Old Testament's typifying of Baptism in the opening prayer. References, however, to the Flood and the crossing of the Red Sea are hardly satisfactory, in spite of their apostolic sanction. They ill accord with the humanity which is the fruit of the Spirit in a Christian Society. The true foreshowing of Baptism is surely the election of the People of God and the establishment with them of the Covenant. Our prayer therefore begins: "Almighty God, thou shepherd of Israel, who didst deliver thy chosen people from the bondage of Egypt, and didst establish with them a sure covenant. ... ." The theme of the shepherd and the flock is prominent in the Mar Thoma Syrian Order of Baptism.

In the lections from the New Testament, just as the dominical Words of Institution are the warrant for the performance of the Eucharist, so too the words of the risen Christ to the Church in Matthew 28: 19 and the teaching of the conversation with Nicodemus (John 3: 5) are the Church's authority for administering Baptism. These two verses are therefore read at the beginning of the exhortation to the people and are followed by a declaration of the Church's intention to baptize:

> Wherefore we are met together to administer Holy Baptism to *these persons* that they may be sealed as *members* of Christ, *Children* of God, and *heirs* of the kingdom of heaven, according to His command.

After this the minister may expound the teaching of Scripture concerning Baptism in his own words. Alternatively to this, and as a guide to such extempore teaching, a series of lections from the teaching of the apostles (Acts 2: 38; Romans 6: 3, 4; 1 Corinthians 12: 13) is given for the Baptism of those able to answer for themselves, and the lection Mark 10: 13–16 for young children and infants. In each case the lections are followed by a brief exhortation inspired by the exhortations in the *Book of Common Order* and the *Book of Common Prayer* (1928).

The lection 1 Corinthians 12: 13 calls for comment; "In one Spirit were we all baptized into one body, whether Jews or Greeks, whether bond or free; and were all made to drink of one Spirit." This verse seemed to the Committee to be crucial for our understanding of the operation of the Spirit in Baptism. It is taken up again as a petition in the litany which precedes the act of Baptism. It enables us to assert that the Spirit is received by infants in Baptism, as well as by believers; for the infant who is baptized is brought into the fellowship of the Church which is created and guided by the Spirit. On the other hand, we must assert that, when the person baptized in infancy grows up and accepts the Christian faith and way of life for himself in Confirmation or reception to full membership of the Church, the Spirit begins to operate in him in a new way. He has made his own that which he was taught by his elders in the Spirit-led community. Confirmation therefore or full membership of the Church is described in the questions put to parents at Infant Baptism and in the final charge at Adult Baptism as being "established in faith by the Holy Spirit".

St. Paul asserts in 1 Corinthians 7: 14 that the children even of a marriage in which only one partner is a believer are "holy", i.e. belonging to God. Indeed, some may claim that through the redemption of the world wrought by Christ this is true of all mankind. The purpose of Infant Baptism is therefore affirmed thus at the end of the exhortation:

> These little children belong with you to God. In Holy Baptism he establishes them in the family and household of faith that they may grow up as members of Christ and heirs of the Kingdom of heaven.

Baptism is a beginning, not an end. And yet the end is realized, so to speak, in advance at this beginning, while still awaiting more complete realization in the future. This is true of the whole of Christian life, which begins and is signified in Baptism. We already are heirs of eternal life, and yet we have to become what we are. This "proleptic" character, as it has been called, of Baptism must find expression in the baptismal order. Already we have referred to children "growing up" as heirs of the kingdom of heaven. In the exhortation at Adult Baptism the final words are a quotation of Philippians 1: 6, which declare to us this same message. "Being confident of this very thing, that he which began a good work in you will perfect it until the day of Jesus Christ."

This same theme is echoed again in the post-baptismal thanksgiving when we pray that the newly baptized "may more and more show forth in their lives that which they now are, by thy grace".

For candidates able to answer for themselves the vows begin with the traditional renunciation of the devil, the world and the flesh. Then follows the profession of faith in the words of the Apostles' Creed in which the whole congregation joins with the candidates, to show that those who have newly believed and confessed that Christ is their Saviour do so in union with the whole believing community and are strengthened in their faith by fellowship with other believers.

The promise to obey God's holy will and commandments follows and is accompanied, in the case of candidates who are husband and wife, by a joint promise to obey Christ's teaching concerning marriage, bring their children to be baptized and instruct them in the Christian faith.

In simple village congregations where candidates may have little or no education, it is sometimes necessary to add supplementary questions of a concrete and particular character to bring home the meaning of the vows they are making. Permission is given for this.

The promises need a conclusion in the form of a blessing and prayer that the candidates may have grace to keep them. The words chosen[1] are derived from the ancient ceremony of the *effeta* (from *ephphatha*) which preceded the renunciation of the devil and was intended as an exorcism. In our baptismal order they come at the end of the promises and are in the form of a blessing which prays that those to be baptized may be delivered from the powers of darkness and may have "their ears open to hear God's voice and their mouths to declare the glory of his name".

In Infant Baptism we had to decide between the traditional promises, similar to those made by adults, and made "in the name of the child" by godparents (or in our case, parents), as in the Anglican rite, and promises made by the parents (and godparents, if any) to bring up their children in the Christian way. After some controversy, mostly outside rather than in the Committee, we decided strongly in favour of the latter, and not a few Anglicans have applauded our decision. Would it be unfair to say that promises made in the name of an infant who knows nothing about them are in the nature of a liturgical fiction, and that promises by parents to fulfil their responsibilities as Christians towards their children are alone in accord with the realities of the

[1] Adapted from A. G. Hebert, *An Essay in Baptismal Revision*, 1947.

situation? The time for promises by the children is later at their Confirmation. The questions to which the parents (and godparents) are required to give answer are translated with some adaptation from the Tamil Methodist Baptism service. So also the final question put to the whole congregation asking them whether they will live in such a way that the children in their midst may grow up in the knowledge and love of God, to which they reply: "We will, God being our helper; and we welcome them into our fellowship."

When the vows have been completed, there is time for silent prayer after which the minister and people greet each other: "The Lord be with you: And with thy Spirit"—to show (as in the Lord's Supper) that a new stage of the service is about to begin.

A new feature at this point is the transposition of the short prayers which precede Baptism in the Anglican and other older rites into litany form, in order to associate the people more closely with the sacramental act.

Water is a natural God-given element which, we may argue, needs no setting apart for the sacramental act for which it is commanded. In any case, to "set apart" a river or a lake for baptism by immersion is hardly possible. Such blessing of the water as there is in the litany follows the ancient Jewish tradition of setting apart with thanksgiving. We give thanks for the creation of water, for Christ's Baptism in Jordan, for His Baptism of suffering and death, for the gift of the Spirit. In the shorter alternative beginning of the litany, thanksgiving is addressed to Father, Son and Holy Spirit in turn. In the suffrages which follow we pray first that those to be baptized may "be born anew in the fellowship of thy Church" and the meaning of this is further expanded in petitions for their continuance in the number of the People of God, their death unto sin and resurrection unto righteousness, their becoming a new creation in Christ, their triumph over evil and their steadfastness in the fruits of the Spirit.

The two final petitions alone can claim to be of Indian origin. They are a "baptizing" of the ancient prayer from the *Upanishads*:

> From the unknown lead us to the known,
> From darkness lead us to light,
> From death lead us to life.

The implication is that this age-long desire of the soul of India finds its true fulfilment in Christian Baptism. In place of this litany the minister may offer prayer in his own words.

The Baptism itself is either by immersion or affusion and according to the Trinitarian formula of universal tradition. It is followed by a declaration: "We have received (i.e. in Baptism) this person (child) into the congregation of Christ's flock. . . ." The signing with the Cross (which Cranmer transferred to this stage from the position before the renunciation which it occupies in the Roman and Lutheran rites) is optional. But whether the signing is given or not, the words adapted from the Anglican rite at this point—"May *these persons* never be ashamed to confess the faith of Christ crucified . . ."—are said for all the newly baptized.

Then the Aaronic blessing may be said or sung, or another hymn of praise, and a procession may be made from the place of Baptism into the body of the church. If the font is at the west end of the church, it may be thought fitting for the minister and the newly baptized to go in procession to the sanctuary steps. But the rubric referred to here is intended to apply chiefly to Baptism by immersion in the open air, after which it is most appropriate to bring the newly baptized to church for thanksgiving and final blessing; and if the Baptism is to be followed immediately by Confirmation and the Lord's Supper, this is a necessity.

The question whether additional ceremonies should be permitted in the service after Baptism engendered no controversy. In many congregations the wearing of new white clothes at Baptism is customary. Thousands of Christians come regularly to Church in white, notably in Travancore, where the custom is universal, and the array of new white clothes on Christmas Day is a distinctive feature of Indian Church life. There are parallel customs amongst non-Christians. Why not therefore give this ceremonial apparelling, according, as it does, with both Indian and ancient Christian traditions, a definite place in the Baptismal liturgy, if desired, to symbolize the new life in Christ? And so we have done.

The only objection came from a missionary working in a poverty-stricken area who said this was a middle-class custom and that the really poor villagers would not be able to afford even the cheapest loin-cloth or sari for their Baptism. We must hope for an Indian society of the future in which such extreme poverty will be done away.

Similarly, the lighting of small earthenware lamps or candles, sometimes from a tall upright brass lamp of Indian design placed in the sanctuary, is a feature of ancient Indian origin which is becoming increasingly popular at the "Family Festival". Here again ancient

Christian and Indian tradition meet, and the newly baptized, holding their lamps or tapers, may be made aware that they are "children of the light". But it is made clear in the introduction that these ceremonies "in no wise add to the efficacy of Baptism, but are intended only to represent the meaning of the sacrament".

The minister then declares that "these our brethren (children) have received the life-giving sign of God's mercy and grace, and have been sealed by the Holy Spirit unto the day of redemption . . ." and goes on to lead the congregation first of all in the Lord's Prayer; for the newly baptized "have received the Spirit of adoption whereby we cry, Abba, Father". Then follows a thanksgiving, taken with some small changes from the Anglican rite, and said by all.

If children have been baptized, the minister adds a prayer for their homes taken from the *Book of Common Prayer* as proposed in 1928.[1] If the newly baptized are adults, a charge is given, either in the minister's own words or as printed, firstly to the congregation, who make a promise to support them with their prayers, encourage them in the Christian life and welcome them into their fellowship; then to the newly baptized themselves, who are reminded briefly of the meaning of their Baptism and of the new life into which they have entered. A hymn may then be sung and the thankoffering is taken.

It is recommended that Baptism should normally take place at a public service of the Church, i.e. at the Lord's Supper or Morning or Evening Prayer. But if it is administered at a separate meeting of the congregation, the people are dismissed with a blessing. In this we have followed the example of *A Proposed Prayer Book* of the Church of India, Pakistan, Burma, and Ceylon, and provided a benediction taken from St. Paul's Prayer in Ephesians 3:

> May God Almighty, the Father of Our Lord Jesus Christ, grant you to be strengthened with power through His Spirit in the inward man; that Christ may dwell in your hearts through faith, and that you may be filled unto all the fulness of God.

---

[1] Adult and Infant Baptism are printed as one order of service with necessary variations appearing in parallel columns.

VI

CHRISTIAN INITIATION—CONFIRMATION

As HAS BEEN pointed out in previous chapters, *The Order of Service for the Reception of Baptized Persons into full Membership of the Church*, commonly called *Confirmation*, was authorized for optional use by the Synod and published in the same year (1950) as the first edition of *The Order for the Lord's Supper*.

The foreword defines the purpose of Confirmation as threefold:

(1) The personal acceptance by the candidate of God's promises, and his personal dedication of himself to Christ as his Lord and Saviour.

(2) Prayer for the increase of the gift of the Holy Spirit.

(3) The reception of the candidate by the congregation into full fellowship of the Church, including especially the fellowship of the Lord's Table.

This last point is to be noted as stressing the important part which the congregation plays in this order of service.

Another paragraph from this foreword is worth quoting as indicating the measure of episcopal authority given and received even when Confirmation is administered by a presbyter:

> Confirmation may be administered, under the Constitution of the Church of South India, by the Bishop, or, in places where this has been the custom, by the presbyter. If a presbyter conducts the service, it is most desirable that he shall be a presbyter appointed by the Bishop, or the presbyter responsible for that congregation.

This should make it clear that it is the intention of C.S.I. to continue episcopal Confirmation where it has been practised before. Indeed, so far from there being any diminution of episcopal Confirmation, it has already become the norm in the majority of the dioceses of the United Church. And where the conviction still holds that a presbyter is the proper minister to perform the rite, he should only perform it—as is fitting in a sacramental action which confers communicant status in the whole Church and not only in the local congregation—when he has due authority to do so.

The foreword also contains recommendations concerning the instruction and examination of the candidates beforehand. The manner and syllabus of instruction vary in different areas of the Church, but in general the Confirmation classes continue for several months and cover the fundamentals of the Creeds and of the Christian way of life.

The liturgical material for the Orders of Baptism and Confirmation is not so fixed in tradition as that belonging to the Eucharist, except for the central acts of Baptism and the laying on of hands. Also there are doubtless few who have given attention to liturgical studies and remain entirely satisfied with any of the existing liturgies of initiation. The drafters of these two Orders have therefore exercised greater freedom than in *The Order for the Lord's Supper* and have considerably adapted and rearranged the material which came to hand, in some cases largely rewriting it. The notification of sources is therefore not easy and is often not of very great importance.

Those familiar with the Anglican order for Confirmation will recognize a general similarity of structure with it and will note that the prayer for the Holy Spirit immediately before the laying on of hands and one of the alternative prayers to be repeated at each laying on of hands are taken with slight alteration from the *Book of Common Prayer*. The fourth question put to the candidates comes from the revised Order for Confirmation of the Church of India, Pakistan, Burma, and Ceylon, and the final blessing from the 1928 Prayer Book. At several points similarity of content indicates that the services for the reception of new members in the *Book of Common Order* and the Methodist *Book of Offices* have been consulted, though there has been radical re-wording of the elements borrowed. A notable borrowing is of the form of reception by the congregation at the end of the service, which comes from the *Book of Common Order* of the United Church of Canada. Part of the introductory exhortation is also from this source.

The service begins with an exhortation which includes the reading of passages of Scripture—a choice of other passages besides Acts 8: 14–17, e.g. John 15: 4–8, and Ephesians 4: 1–6. There is an alternative shorter introduction which bishops and presbyters, anxious not to weary the candidates and congregation, may well elect to read more often than the longer one. But it is to be hoped that, even if the latter is not read in the service, it will be used in catechetical instruction. There can be few finer statements than that contained in it of the meaning of the gift of the Spirit.

After this an address may be given, and the minister then calls upon the candidates to stand and make their profession of faith and solemn promise to live the Christian life. The questions to which they have to give answer are more searching and specific than the ones with which Anglicans are familiar. At the end of the questions the names of the candidates are read out one by one and each candidate makes his or her promise individually, reaffirming the promises already made corporately in the words: "I do, God being my helper."

The vows are completed by a silent confession of sin and a profoundly moving act of self-dedication which the candidates say after the minister. This is a translation of a passage found in the same position and with the same intent in the Tamil Methodist service for reception of baptized persons into full membership of the Church.

The act of laying on of hands is preceded by silent prayer and a prayer for the gift of the Holy Spirit, taken with some alteration from the Anglican rite and said either by the minister (bishop or presbyter) alone, or by the whole congregation together with him.

Three alternative forms of words are given for the laying on of hands. The first is adapted from St. Paul's prayer in Ephesians 3, the second and third are adaptations of the Anglican prayer at the same point. This is perhaps an example of the way in which we have tended in our experimental editions of services to give more alternatives than are really necessary. No doubt the verdict of bishops and presbyters who have used the service will guide us in our choice of one or two of these in the revised edition, though our principle is to allow, where possible, for a measure of freedom and variety.

There may be a presentation, either here or at the end of the service, of a membership card and a Prayer Book, Bible or New Testament to each candidate. When the act of Confirmation is completed, all join in saying the Lord's Prayer and the minister adds a post-Confirmation prayer:

> . . . Let thy fatherly hand, we beseech thee, be over them: let thy Holy Spirit ever be with them: and so lead them in the knowledge and obedience of thy word that they may serve thee all their days and be with thee for ever. . . .

The reception of the newly confirmed by the congregation with which the service ends is as much an efficacious sign as the laying on of hands. In fact the C.S.I. order has two climaxes which give it a double theological emphasis. The minister, be he bishop or presbyter, acts as representative of the universal Church and in the name of Christ who bestowed the Spirit upon His disciples. The members of the congregation present are also representative of the universal Church, in that they are the *ecclesia* of God in that place. The primary manifestation of the fruit of the Spirit, according to the New Testament, is within the fellowship of the local Church. Part of our understanding of the gift of the Spirit in Confirmation must be that it signifies entrance into the fulness of membership in the Spirit-guided community. Hence the sacramental completion of the act of laying on of hands in the act of reception.

The newly confirmed rise and face the congregation and the latter stand and together address them, affectionately welcoming them into full fellowship, renewing their vows together with them, and pledging to them their sympathy, help and prayers.

The newly confirmed then turn and face the minister again, who declares that they have been received into the full fellowship of the Church and exhorts them to fight manfully under the banner of Christ, or he may give them the right hand of fellowship or "they may greet each other in any appropriate manner". This latter alternative is included for the sake of the many village Christians who are not accustomed to the European manner of shaking hands and might, in particular, think it strange for a minister to take the right hand of one of the opposite sex.

The blessing "Go forth into the world in peace . . ." is taken from the Prayer Book as proposed in 1928. Alternative to it is the ascription, "Now unto him that is able to keep you from falling. . . ."

It is recommended that the Lord's Supper should be celebrated at the same time, and the newly confirmed receive communion together before the rest of the congregation. In this event, Confirmation takes place after the Litany of Intercession in *The Order for the Lord's Supper*, and the newly confirmed make their offerings at the time of the offertory, which follows immediately after the Order for Confirmation.

If there is no such celebration of the Lord's Supper, the blessing of the newly confirmed is followed by a hymn during which the offerings are received. There may be an address and the minister dismisses the people with a blessing.

We have already noted that both the Orders for Baptism and for Confirmation are at an experimental stage and the experience of use has already revealed some points at which revision seems desirable. Perhaps the author, who has in the past been given the task of collecting comments on and criticisms of the products of the Liturgy Committee, may be permitted to add that suggested improvements are most welcome from any quarter. While we greatly value the help we have received and hope still to receive from liturgists, the comments of parochial ministers and the laity have a practical value of their own.

N.B. The next Chapter (VII) was written before September 1957. For a report of the work of the Synod Liturgy Committee since then see Appendix (p. 59).

VII

TOWARDS A C.S.I. PRAYER BOOK

AT PRESENT THE only service books, either in English or the four South Indian languages, which are available in one volume for ministers and laity, are those which were already in use in the uniting Churches before union, i.e. the Anglican *Book of Common Prayer*, *The Directory of Worship* of the former South India United Church (Congregationalist and Presbyterian) and the Methodist *Book of Offices*. This in itself has been a factor encouraging the continued use of the forms of worship contained in them as the norm in most congregations. The various C.S.I. Orders have been published so far in separate booklets which individual worshippers can hardly be expected to purchase for themselves. Not many congregations have the funds available to provide them in church, and even those which have may have hesitated to do so in view of the fact that most of the Orders are still in experimental editions, liable to more or less radical revision in the not very distant future.

Undoubtedly, therefore, the publication of a C.S.I. prayer book is much to be desired. Its availability will at once provide an incentive for the regular use of the services contained in it, though congregations will still be at liberty to continue in the use of the older prayer books. Various factors, however, have militated against the hastening of publication. In the first place, those competent to undertake the task of drafting the orders of worship are all busy men, heavily involved in episcopal, pastoral or educational responsibilities; and the C.S.I. has been too short of qualified leadership to be able to release any of them entirely for this work. They have had to snatch precious hours for it in the midst of other duties, or make it a series of holiday tasks.

Also, the radical re-examination of existing liturgical forms, both ancient and modern, which a united Church must undertake if it is to be true to its destiny, is a task which cannot be completed in a hurry. If the revisions of the Anglican *Book of Common Prayer* or the Scottish *Book of Common Order*, within the English and Scottish liturgical traditions respectively, have taken a decade, or even a generation, to complete, *a fortiori* the liturgical task of C.S.I. must take a long time. And it would hardly be fair on the members of our congregations, the majority of whom have to make some sacrifice to buy a prayer book, if they can afford it at all, to publish prematurely a collection of experimental Orders which would later become obsolete. The work must therefore go on in its present manner for a few more years.

In this chapter some account must be given both of what has already been done in addition to the sacramental orders outlined in previous chapters, and of what still remains to be done.

1. Calendar and Lectionary

Mention has already been made in writing about the lections in the Order for the Eucharist[1] of the three booklets, *Daily Bible Readings* (1954), *Bible Readings and Collects for Sundays and Other Special Days, with Proper Prefaces* (1954), and *Additional Bible Readings and Collects for Sundays and Other Special Days* (1956). The inconvenience of having these in three separate booklets has had to be endured for the sake of publishing each section of the work as it has been completed. It will no doubt disappear when the experimental period gives place to the definitive edition, and the whole Calendar and Lectionary is published in one volume or included in the awaited C.S.I. prayer book. Already the revision of the *Daily Bible Readings* is well on its way towards completion. Also from Advent 1954 onwards all the Bible readings have been conveniently available in an annually published almanack, cheap enough for all to buy.

The purpose of the daily readings is twofold. It is a lectionary for use at Morning and Evening Prayer, where these are read daily in church: it is also intended for private devotional use. A measure of not entirely resolved tension is discernible between the desire to provide readings short enough for the capacity of the average layman and the aim of including all the passages in the Bible which ought to be read during the course of the year. Perhaps the difficulty of deciding which principle should prevail is inevitable. The lections in the other two booklets are primarily intended for reading at the Eucharist; but they also serve as alternative or additional private reading on the days concerned.

2. A Covenant Service[2]

The solemn reaffirmation of our covenant with God through Jesus

---

[1] P. 23.

[2] *Order of Service for such as would enter into or renew their Covenant with God, for use on the first Sunday of the year or other occasion,* 1956.

Christ in an act of self-dedication at the beginning of each year is a Methodist tradition which goes back to John Wesley himself. Indeed, Wesley's Covenant Service must be accorded the status of a classic in the literature of Christian devotion. There have been modifications of it published from time to time; but a form very close to the original has been widely used in South India, and the Diocese of Medak published a revision of this in 1952. Those not of the Methodist heritage who were asked to comment on this form of service, after studying it in some cases for the first time, were in general of the opinion that it was an admirable manual for private devotion and might serve for a corporate act of self-dedication at a retreat for ministers or Church workers, but that it made too great demands on the individual worshipper to be suitable for use in most congregations. There were those of the Methodist heritage too who agreed with this view. Moreover, the Methodist Church in England had published a form more suited to general use in 1936. It was this latter which was used as a basis for the C.S.I. form with such revision as the Liturgy Committee considered desirable.[1]

The climax of the order is the solemn affirmation of the Covenant. After an exhortation by the minister, during which the people stand, all kneel and the minister prays:

> O Lord God, Holy Father, who hast called us through Christ to be partakers in this gracious Covenant, we take upon ourselves with joy the yoke of obedience, and engage ourselves, for love of thee, to seek and do thy perfect will. We are no longer our own, but thine.

Here all the people join:

> I am no longer my own, but thine. Put me to what thou wilt, rank me with whom thou wilt; put me to doing, put me to suffering; let me be employed for thee or laid aside for thee, exalted for thee or brought low for thee; let me be full, let me be empty; let me have all things, let me have nothing; I freely and heartily yield all things to thy pleasure and disposal.
>
> And now, O glorious and blessed God, Father, Son and Holy Spirit, thou art mine and I am thine. So be it. And the Covenant which I have made on earth, let it be ratified in heaven. Amen.

This is preceded by acts of adoration, thanksgiving and confession in litany form, a collect and lections (Jeremiah 31: 31–33, Hebrews 12: 22–25a, Matthew 11: 27–30). It will be noticed that the distinctive feature of this order of service, in which it differs most markedly from

[1] *Op. cit.*, p. iii.

its Methodist prototypes, is that the general framework is assimilated to that of the first two parts of *The Order for the Lord's Supper*. It is recommended in the Introduction (p. iv) that it be used, on the occasions for which it is appointed, as an alternative for this earlier part of the eucharistic rite and completed, wherever possible, by "the Breaking of the Bread", beginning at the Offertory Sentences. If this be done, the order for the renewal of the Covenant ends with a period of silence, and the Offertory Sentences are preceded by a versicle and response:

> Jesus said: This cup is the New Covenant in my blood, even that which is poured out for you.
> Praise be to Thee, O Christ.

New Year's Day has for long been an occasion for devout self-oblation in every congregation in South India, and in many churches, particularly those of the Anglican heritage, midnight celebrations of the Eucharist are as well attended as those at Christmas and Easter. This provision, therefore, of a renewal of the Covenant in connexion with the Eucharist is likely to meet a liturgical need. If there is no celebration, the service ends with the Lord's Prayer, a hymn, during which offerings are received, and an ascription of glory to the Triune God. The likelihood of its being acceptable to the heirs of other traditions than the Methodist is evidenced by the fact that its first use in the official Tamil translation occurred at a conference of ministers in the ex-Anglican Diocese of Tinnevelly immediately before the Diocesan Council. The form of service had to be rushed through the press to be ready for it.

3. *The Ordinal*

The united Church at its inauguration could not have operated to replenish its ministry without accepted orders for the ordination of deacons and presbyters and the consecration of bishops. Indeed, the consecration of nine new bishops immediately followed the inauguration. An ordinal was therefore prepared and approved by the Negotiating Committee before union and has been used invariably ever since.

It has been accepted in the dioceses without much articulate criticism; but there are some difficulties in it which have made it advisable to follow the same principle as with other services and submit it to revision after a few years of use. The reason why this has not been done before is that other assignments to the Liturgy Committee seemed more urgent.

The main point at which revision is desirable is the accommodation of all three Ordination Services to the C.S.I. *Order for the Lord's Supper.* They were published three years before the latter, and their framework is that of the Anglican Ordinal; so that they fit most easily into the Anglican Order for Holy Communion. The C.S.I. liturgy is now almost invariably used at ordinations and has been used without exception at consecrations of bishops; but the manner of fitting the Ordination Services into it has varied considerably and has not always been happy.

Nor is it the framework alone which is of Anglican origin. The whole ordinal is very largely the Anglican one with such minor revisions as were already approved or at the time contemplated in the Anglican province of India, Pakistan, Burma, and Ceylon. Other denominational traditions in the matter were hardly considered. This in itself is not necessarily an objection, as in C.S.I. we have moved beyond any rivalry between the heirs of the former denominations (except in a few tiresome local situations). In consequence there is no need in our liturgical construction to make sure that we have conserved an even balance between the differing liturgical heritages. Rather we aim at discovering what seems to us the right expression of our worship at any particular point, whatever its confessional origin may be.

At the same time, it has never proved to be the case that one heritage has everything and the others nothing; and in this particular liturgical task the Ordinal of the Church of Scotland outstandingly demanded consideration. Its ordination prayer, the central point of the service, is in many respects more primitive in structure and more acceptable to liturgists than the Anglican one. Other orders which have attracted our attention are those in the *Book of Common Order* of the United Church of Canada and the Congregationalist *Book of Public Worship.*

A draft of the services for deacons and presbyters, embodying a fairly conservative revision, was printed for study by the Liturgy Committee in 1955. At about the same time a sub-committee of the Negotiating Committee for Church Union in North India and Pakistan was working on an ordinal for the proposed united Churches and decided in favour of using the Ordination Service for Presbyters in *The Ordinal and Service Book* of the Church of Scotland as the basis for their drafting. A member of the C.S.I. Liturgy Committee happened to be staying in North India at the time and was invited to attend this sub-committee as a consultant. This proved to be the beginning of an unofficial but fruitful liaison between those working on this task of liturgical construction in the South and in the North. The immediate result of this collaboration has been the acceptance by the Liturgy Committee in September 1956 of a draft ordinal which is substantially the same, as far as the ordination of presbyters is concerned, as the draft service approved by the North Indian Negotiating Committee in April 1957. The proposed C.S.I. orders for the ordination of deacons and the consecration of bishops are constructed, *mutatis mutandis*, on the same lines.

In North India and in Pakistan the draft has to be submitted along with the plans of Church Union to the negotiating Churches, while the South Indian draft has to face another scrutiny by the Liturgy Committee in September 1957 and a debate in Synod in 1958. It is therefore too early at the time of writing to give a detailed account of it. Very briefly, the services are in the main a conflation of material derived from the Ordinal of the Church of Scotland with the C.S.I. Ordinal, as already revised in 1955, with considerable working over and revision of the whole, including the addition of phrases and sentences from other sources. Most encouraging praise of this draft has been received from the liturgists of more than one communion, including the Anglican. The mention of the approval of Anglican liturgical experts is intended to allay the anxieties of those Anglicans who feared that a revision of our ordinal might be for the worse rather than for the better!

The question most debated at the moment (other criticisms and suggestions being mostly in favour of minor emendations) is whether the act of ordination with laying on of hands should take place during the Ordination Prayer, as in the primitive ordinals, or with a separate ordination formula addressed to the candidate as in the Roman and Anglican rites. The former undoubtedly has the support of expert liturgiological opinion; but the latter has some practical considerations to commend it. No issue of doctrine or order is involved; and it is not without significance that those who would advocate the retention of the separate formula in the Anglican mode, if not precisely with the Anglican wording, are as likely to be Congregationalist or Methodist in their upbringing as Anglican.

Mention must also be made of *The Order of Service for the Commissioning of Sisters in the C.S.I.*, i.e. admitting them to the C.S.I.

Order of Women which is the equivalent of the Order of Deaconesses in other communions. Though this was not drafted by the Liturgy Committee, it has been examined by it and sanctioned for experimental use.

The commissioning takes place during a celebration of the Lord's Supper. After the Creed, the candidates are presented to the Bishop, who delivers a homily and examines them briefly as to their calling to membership of the Order, their faith and their acceptance of the common rule of the Order. Each candidate in turn then makes a solemn profession of faith and promise of obedience. After a period of silence the prayer of commissioning follows, and each candidate in turn kneels before the Bishop, who presents her with a Bible and the Cross of the Order, saying: "By the authority of the Church of South India I admit you as a Sister of the Church." This is followed by a blessing of each candidate, and, when all have been admitted, a hymn is sung. The celebration of the Lord's Supper then proceeds with special suffrages for the Order and the newly admitted Sisters in the Litany.

4. Other work, planned or already in progress

(a) *Morning and Evening Prayer.* There has been no urgent need for constructional work on the services of Morning and Evening Prayer. The Anglican orders have continued in use unchanged in congregations of Anglican origin, while those of other heritages have preferred a mainly non-liturgical tradition of congregational worship, though seldom without some liturgical elements.

In view of the fact that before union the different denominational heritages seldom overlapped, except in the cities, and were established in separate districts, mostly of the size of English counties, it would be possible for these traditions of worship to continue without mutual influence to the end of time, and many a conservative village congregation would rather have it so. On the other hand, creativity and development is to be expected in a united Church here as elsewhere. The author has had personal experience of experimentation in the chapel of one of our theological colleges with a liturgical framework predominantly that of the Anglican Morning and Evening Prayer and following the C.S.I. lectionary and an ordered reading of Psalms, but at the same time allowing greater freedom and elasticity within this framework. Already in its revised Prayer Books,[1] the Anglican Com-

[1] E.g. The Prayer Book as Proposed in 1928 and *The Proposed Prayer Book* of the C.I.P.B.C. (1951).

munion has moved in this direction and given permission to use extempore prayer after the Third Collect as well as providing a wider anthology of printed intercessions and thanksgiving. Unfortunately few of the congregations of the Anglican heritage in South India have ventured to make full use of this liberty accorded to them even before union. The old familiar collects are generally as magnificent in their South Indian translations as in the sixteenth-century originals, but there is often undue formality and rigidity in their use. On the other hand, prayer in the extempore tradition can often be deficient in the broader vision of the Church and the loftier understanding of its worship.

In this situation clearly some guidance is needed and the projected C.S.I. Prayer Book would be incomplete without it. At the present stage of inquiry and drafting the trend of opinion is that while there must be some mutual influence in the two ways of public worship, liturgical and extempore, we should not attempt to fuse them into one order, but rather allow for a wide measure of variety.

If there is to be any fusion, it may be found in an already accepted provision for Morning Prayer, i.e. that where a celebration of the Eucharist is impossible, the first two parts of *The Order for the Lord's Supper* may be used as an Order for public worship. There is room in this order for wide variety, including the use of extempore prayer in place of the litany of intercession. This recommendation, however, does not appear to have been widely followed.

Partly in deference to popular preference for existing forms, but not without an appreciation of the value of these forms and the desirability that they should be preserved for posterity, the Committee is at work (a) on a revision of the Anglican Orders of Morning and Evening Prayer; (b) on a "free" Order of public worship with the Orders given in Presbyterian and Congregationalist directories of worship as its exemplars. At the present stage of drafting it may be predicted that the former Order, which will be in line with the Anglican tradition, will introduce the Syrian *Kauma* (invocation of the Trinity) as an opening act of adoration. It will also allow for greater elasticity and variety, including the interchange of some of the canticles at Morning and Evening Prayer. In many churches one of these is the main service of the day attended by the majority of Christians in the locality, while the other draws only a handful of worshippers. In general it is the morning service which is most popular, while on a Sunday evening many prefer to meet together in prayer cells at different houses. Such congregations seldom sing the Magnificat, unless, as may now be recommended, it is sometimes sung at Morning Prayer.

The Synod Liturgy Committee expects that considerable freedom will be exercised by the liturgy committees of the linguistic areas in adapting to local needs and conditions the translations of these proposed forms of service and the others discussed below. There is also considerable scope here for the much needed introduction into worship of Indian forms of prayer and hymnody.

(b) *Admission to the Catechumenate.* One liturgist has criticized us for not working on this simultaneously with the Order for Baptism and Confirmation. There were, of course, various forms for the admission of catechumens in use in the uniting Churches before union, and these have continued in use since union. They need, however, to be critically examined and a revised form drafted which is properly related to the C.S.I. *Order for Holy Baptism.*

(c) *Form of admission to the C.S.I. of Christians already baptized.* It is contrary to the *ethos* of the C.S.I. to proselytize amongst the adherents of other communions. In any case, Christians belonging to communions which are in comity (i.e. co-operation rather than competition) with the C.S.I. and which accept the Bible, the Apostles' and Nicene Creeds and the two Sacraments of the Gospel are free to declare themselves members of the C.S.I., if resident in South India, and are accepted, according to their status, whether as baptized persons or as communicants.

It does, however, sometimes happen that members of Christian communions not in comity with the C.S.I., and whose beliefs and practices may in some respects be contrary to the C.S.I. Basis of Union, wish to leave their old allegiance and become members of our Church. Some form of inquiry into their orthodoxy and welcome into our fellowship is desirable and an Order for this is in process of drafting.

(d) *The Communion of the Sick.* Although those who have used the C.S.I. *Order of the Lord's Supper* in administering communion to the sick have probably not found great difficulty in accommodating previously existing directives to the new Order, clearly C.S.I. must have its own recommendations, and these are being drafted.

(e) *Marriages* are still solemnized and *burials* conducted according to the various orders in use since before union and the task of drafting C.S.I. Orders has still to be undertaken. There are a number of occasional offices, such as the dedication of a church building, the blessing of a new house, and the Harvest Festival, which in rural congregations has become one of the great occasions of the Church's year. For all these provision will have to be made after examination and, if need be, revision of existing usages.

The last mentioned, the Harvest Festival, is a fitting symbol of the all-embracing character at which Christian worship must aim. The characteristic harvest thanksgiving of South India is seldom as decorative as its Western counterpart, but much more realistic. In the central part of the thanksgiving service chickens, kids and calves, as well as baskets of rice and other vegetable products are brought up by each donor in procession and solemnly presented to the presiding minister. The sale of this produce may very well form a substantial part of the church's income. It all symbolizes and declares the truth that God is not merely the God of the sanctuary—if He were, He would be less than the God revealed in the Bible—but the God of the plough, the irrigation reservoir and the rice mill. The world of nature and all man's daily activities in the use of its resources belong to Him. Our offering of the fruit of our daily labour, linked as it is with our praises for creation and redemption, is an acknowledgment that God is the Lord of all life and that our true worship is to consecrate all to Him.

APPENDIX

THE WORK OF THE LITURGY COMMITTEE IN SEPTEMBER 1957, AS APPROVED BY THE SYNOD IN JANUARY 1958

1. *Public worship other than the Lord's Supper.* Provision had already been made for an optional use of the first two parts of *An Order for the Lord's Supper* as a service of public worship on Sundays or other days when for any reason the Lord's Supper is not to be celebrated. While it is hoped that this practice may grow, the traditions which prevailed at the time of union have continued in use, and the Liturgy Committee has thought fit to give its approval to this variety and at the same time to guide the congregations towards an enrichment of their worship. The preparatory work for this was entrusted to the Dioceses of Tirunelveli (Tinnevelly) and South Travancore, strongholds respectively of the Anglican and Congregationalist heritages. The result has been the publication of a booklet the full title of which is, *An Order for Morning and Evening Prayer* and *A Service of Worship with An Outline for Public Worship* (1958).

There are three alternative orders.

The first is based on the orders for Morning and Evening Prayer in the Anglican *Book of Common Prayer.* New features are: (a) the use of the Syrian *Kauma,* or invocation of the Trinity as an opening act of adoration, (b) a reordering of other versicles and responses, (c) the use of part of Psalm 51 as one of three alternative forms of Confession, (d) permission to transpose the canticles (the wording of which has in a few places been revised) from Morning to Evening Prayer and *vice versa,* "if on any day there is only one service in church", (e) the placing of the *Te Deum* after the second lesson, (f) a greater elasticity in the intercessions after the third collect.

The second order, drafted in South Travancore, is surprisingly similar to the first in general outline and incorporates items familiar to users of the Anglican Prayer Book, such as the General Confession, General Thanksgiving and Prayer of St. Chrysostom. It would have been possible to conflate these two orders, which represent the mutual influence of the Anglican and "Free" Church heritages in South India both before and since union; but it was decided to let them stand side by side, for the present. A third outline is added for those who prefer a "free" type of service. This booklet was authorized immediately by the Synod Executive Committee without presentation to the Synod. The intention is that it should be translated freely into Tamil by the Tamil dioceses which prepared it and that other language areas should be permitted to make their own adaptations of it.

2. *The Ordinal.*[1] The chief sources for the revision now approved by the Synod are the Ordinal of the Church of Scotland and the Anglican Ordinal as mediated through the C.S.I. Ordinal of 1947. The three orders for the ordination of Deacons, the ordination of Presbyters and the consecration of Bishops all follow substantially the same pattern. The ordination takes place during the course of the celebration of the Lord's Supper. The candidates (or Bishop-elect) are presented to the Bishop after the Confession and Declaration of Forgiveness. The authorization of the diocese for their ordination is read and the Bishop presents them to the assembled people, who give a response of assent to the ordination.

The Collect, Lessons, Sermon and Nicene Creed follow, after which the candidates are examined in a series of questions which make clear the nature and functions of each order of the ministry and the way of life expected of those who participate in it.

After silent prayer and a hymn of prayer to the Holy Spirit, the Bishop (together with the Presbyters who lay on hands with him in Presbyters' ordination, and the Bishops and Presbyters who take part with him in episcopal consecration) stands and says the Ordination Prayer. The first part of the prayer is a glorification of God for His revelation of Himself in Jesus Christ, in Deacon's ordination stress being laid on Christ's coming to serve, in that of Presbyters and Bishops on His High Priesthood and gift of the ministry for the building up of the Church. The second part of the prayer, "Send down thy Holy Spirit upon thy servant . . .", is repeated with laying on of hands for each ordinand. The third and concluding part of the prayer consists of petition for the gifts of the Spirit appropriate to each order of the ministry. This form of ordination prayer is commended as theologic-ally preferable to the formula "Receive the Holy Spirit . . ." addressed to the ordinand and as liturgically in accord with primitive models. The repetition of the central part of the prayer has the practical advan-

[1] To be published by O.U.P.

tage of enabling the laying on of hands to take place during the ordination prayer and not apart from it, as in Roman and Anglican ordinations, without necessitating the laying on of hands throughout the entire prayer and the repetition of the whole of it for each candidate, as in Eastern ordinations, if the rubrics are followed.

The presentation of a Bible follows in all ordinations and the giving of the right hand of fellowship. A pastoral staff is also presented to a newly consecrated Bishop. Finally the Bishop declares "that . . . are Deacons (Presbyters, Bishops) in the Church of God, in the name of the Father and of the Son and of the Holy Spirit". This corresponds with the declaration in Eastern ordinals. The people respond with a doxology and the Order of the Lord's Supper continues from the Litany. The act of ordination is thus set in the framework of the assent, prayer and thanksgiving of the people.

3. *The Office for Making a Catechumen.*[1]

4. *A Service for the Reception into the Church of South India of Baptized and Communicant Members from Other Churches.*[1]

These are both simple short services beginning with question and answer and leading to prayer. The latter is only intended for use in the case of members of Churches not in comity with the C.S.I. who wish for good reason to transfer their allegiance.

5. *Directions for the Communion of the Sick.* Two ways are authorized: either a shortened celebration in the sick room or the taking of bread and wine which have been set apart in a celebration in church, as soon as convenient, to the sick of the parish.

6. *Future Tasks.* The Synod instructs the newly appointed Committee (i) to prepare orders for Marriage and Burial, (ii) to complete the revision of the lectionary, (iii) to revise Baptism and Confirmation, (iv) to work towards the publication of the first part of the C.S.I. Prayer Book.

[1] At present only published in English in the Synod Report.

INDEX